I AM AMAZING

How I Transformed Trauma Into Happiness & Broke Free from the Past

JENNIFER W. STERLING

Unless otherwise specified, all definitions were obtained from Oxford Languages (Google).

Unless otherwise specified, all Bible quotations are from the ERV.

www.jenslifecoaching.com

www.jenniferwsterling.com

Contents

To Ethan, Emmalee, and Jackson. You are my greatest creations and you have taught me so much. I love you all equally and unconditionally. Never stop believing in your potential.

To my Aunt Erin and Grandmother Kay. Thank you for being the moms I needed when my mom couldn't. I am who I am today partly because of you both. I love you.

To my extended family. May we all continue to heal and break cycles for generations to come.

To my coaches, therapists, and peers. Without your guidance, wisdom, and support, I would not be here today.

To my dad. I wish I were able to know you better. I love you and I forgive you.

To my mom. I miss you more than my words can ever express. I think of you every single day and wish you were here. I am sorry for all the times I was an asshole. Thank you for being the best grandmother "Banga" to my babies. They sure did love you.

Introduction

There is one thing you should know about writing. It will inevitably lead you to dark places, as you cannot write authentically about something unless you have lived it ... But do not be too indulgent despite how addictive sadness can be ... You must emerge from adversity, scathed but victorious, to tell your story and, in turn, light the way for others.

Lang Leav

I keep that quote on the corkboard above my laptop. While writing this book, sometimes the simplest memory or sentence would cause me to cry. Self-destruction and suffering can be addictive, just like drugs, alcohol, and gambling. What started off a couple of years ago as a memoir about my experience with narcissistic and sexual abuse turned into a loving, healing journey for my soul and for my children's souls, as well as the souls of my parents, who are no longer with us.

This book has been forty-five years in the making, and the writing of it has taken me back to some dark places. But my story is meant to be told, regardless of who does or doesn't read it. I can't worry about that. What matters to me is that it's the healing voice to my past. It's an outlet for the little girl inside me to be seen and heard and validated—by herself—without fear of others' judgments or opinions. It's breaking generational cycles on both sides of my family, healing the past, and creating a new path for my children and their children.

> *A woman who heals herself heals her mother, her daughter, and every woman around her.*
>
> Unknown

Sharing my story through this book also matters because it provides one more channel reminding us all that we are not alone. For the sake of those who may be silent because they believe the wounds inflicted on them were just not severe enough to warrant raising their voices, I have written my story. Regardless of whether the trauma they've sustained rises to the level where they might feel justified to speak up, the damage they've incurred may be weighing them down and holding them back from a happy life. And not feeling free to talk about what they've been through just leaves them feeling alone. I hope reading my story will be inspiring for those who may be feeling like they are never going to be genuinely happy. I am here to tell you that it's never too late to find intrinsic happiness.

I remember writing short stories and mini-books by hand as a young girl in middle school. That's when I first knew I wanted to publish a book. As I got older, I would use my beloved typewriter. Eventually, I took online writing courses. I thought I would end up writing fictional stories based on my fears and desires, and that I would be able to hide behind my characters. I never would have believed my first book would be a transformational memoir/self-help book. Could I allow myself to be that exposed and vulnerable?

My book does not offer groundbreaking information, but it's real. It's authentic. I am human, just like you, just like the rest of the world. I often say, "Humans are stupid," meaning *Sometimes we are our own worst enemies*. We don't know what we don't know, and consequently, we make some big mistakes, not to mention thousands of little ones.

I have made plenty of mistakes in my life, some that filled me with guilt and shame for years. And while those mistakes are not my proudest moments, they have been learning experiences. I no longer feel ashamed or guilty about my past errors in judgment. Going further, I forgive all those who have hurt me as well. And oddly enough, I am grateful for those lessons and experiences ... even the traumatic ones.

I have three amazing children, and I was a stay-at-home mom for many years. And yet, during that time, I believed that I lost myself. Eventually, I learned that was not the case but only because I had never found myself to begin with. I carried my pain and trauma inside, and I suppressed whatever I could manage, truly believing that was the answer. I told myself, *If I don't think about my pain anymore, I must be past it, right?* Wrong.

Suppression: *a choice a person makes to remove thoughts or feelings from one's conscious awareness*

Suppressed pain will always haunt us and rear its ugly head. It must be dealt with if we want to live a happy life. There is no other way. And it must be done from the inside out.

Now I am in my forties, and I have found myself. I have not only begun the exhausting, beneficial, and never-ending journey of healing my past, but also have found my life's purpose. My purpose is helping others heal and find their purpose. Without purpose, life has no meaning, and we aren't truly happy.

What Is a Purpose?

Many of us assume that having a purpose or focusing on goals or pursuing anything meant to lead to success always centers around a desire for career enhancement or making money. That is 100 percent false! I enjoy working with stay-at-home moms, helping them find their purpose AND get a job but *only* if a new job happens to be their goal. Our purpose in our current season can be anything, even if that's just to be happy right where we are.

Sadly, not everyone wants to be happy. But most of us do, and that doesn't mean we have to be a top CEO or a business guru to find happiness. In fact, most CEOs and business gurus aren't all that happy. As you will hear me say over and over, happiness comes from within.

I use the word *intrinsic* a lot because, for whatever reason, I attach that word to my core. It's what is there and will never go away. We can suppress awareness of our intrinsic value and cause ourselves to suffer, even to be miserable. Suffering can become a *habit,* a friendly word for addiction. We can literally become addicted to abusing ourselves. And when we do that, the world will follow our lead.

Intrinsic: *Belonging to the essential nature or constitution of a thing*
Examples: the intrinsic worth of a gem, or the intrinsic brightness of a star

—Merriam-Webster

Having intrinsic value means we can love ourselves organically and unconditionally. We all have intrinsic value and worth, whether or not we choose to see it. Intrinsic happiness is the ONLY successful way to be happy. I cannot express that enough. External factors can definitely bring us joy, but relying on them to be happy is a recipe for depression and anxiety.

Who Am I?

I am a woman who's been at the top, the bottom, and everywhere in between. You and I may not have experienced the same events or traumas, but I have been in your shoes. I've lived with overwhelming feelings of loneliness and abandonment. The heartbreak of a broken marriage and the fear of being alone have preyed on my sense of self-confidence. I've struggled as a married mom and as a single mom. The premature loss of both my parents due to their unhealthy addictions and habits has filled me with sadness.

My adult weight has fluctuated from 107 pounds to 170, and no matter what my size, I have felt uncomfortable in my skin for most of my life. I used to look in the mirror and endlessly criticize myself, berating every aspect of my appearance. The bags under my eyes ... my frizzy hair ... my uneven complexion ... my fat-ass body. My crooked smile and those damned crow's feet! My inner dialogue was a barrage of self-judging commentary, and I didn't let others off the hook, either. As a result, I would build nothing but resentment and angry emotions within myself.

Although I believed myself to be a good person, I didn't feel worthy of love. I didn't express my love to its fullest extent, and I couldn't truly accept love from others, no matter how desperately I wanted to. I tolerated mistreatment from so many people—at my jobs, in society at large, and even within my inner circle.

> *When you give yourself a high five, it is impossible to think something crappy about yourself.*
>
> Mel Robbins

After starting my healing journey and then doing the hard work for years, I no longer beat myself up internally, not even when sizing myself up at the mirror. It has not been easy, especially not in the beginning. But for the first time in my life, I truly love myself. I no longer seek external validation for who I am as a woman, a mother, or a partner, or for my accomplishments. I am not saying I am always centered and Gandhi-like; however, my bad days are limited and are more like bad moments.

I am a private person by nature. My having written this book will be a shock to a lot of people who had no idea it was even a desire of mine. But healing ourselves is a forever process, and that is true whether our past was highly traumatic or pretty perfect. Writing this book was probably one of the hardest things I have ever chosen to do. I made that choice because, after years of pain and struggle, I feel amazing and happy, and I want the whole world to feel amazing and happy.

Today, I am a certified both as a life coach and a health coach (two different certifications). I help others live an intrinsically happy life starting with how they feed their mind and how they feed their body. I am not a nutritionist, and I can't create meal plans. But I can help my clients live the healthy lifestyle they choose. Maybe they choose to live gluten-free or want to exercise more. I can help them evaluate what they are eating or how they are exercising in order to ensure they are effectively implementing their choices. Or as one of my instructors at school describes it, "A health coach can provide the right system, accountability, and support for the new 'lifestyle prescription' from a doctor."

Doc says, *exercise more, eat less, drink less alcohol, stop smoking, drink more water, take your vitamins* ... Doc then moves on to the next patient. As a health coach with specialized training in habit change, I can help you follow your doctor's orders. As a life coach with specialized knowledge in psychology and human behavior, I can help you create new internal habits at a sustainable pace that opens the door to intrinsic happiness. No matter what crap life throws at us (and it will because that's life), having intrinsic happiness and self-worth gets us through the mess with more ease and less suffering.

> *Life isn't about waiting for the storm to pass ... it's learning to dance in the rain.*
>
> Vivian Greene

In this book, I share some private information from MY experiences that not many people know about. I share my story not only to give the little girl inside me a voice but also to maybe crack open the playroom door for someone else's inner child who is dying to be heard. We all have a past. And we all have to deal with that past in order to find inner peace and happiness.

I do not use names in this book, although sometimes the identities are unavoidably clear by their close relationship to me. Many events I choose to share sucked. Some that are worse, I have chosen not to share. In relating my experiences, to the best of my ability, I have minimized the sharing of details of my interactions with various individuals, both to remain respectful of them and to avoid drama in my life.

How to Use This Book

I set up this book in a way that doesn't require it to be read cover to cover for someone to find it useful. Each chapter can be read or referenced according to individual preferences, as needed. I take note of a lot of definitions because I have learned that often, many of us don't really understand the definition of a word. Getting to the specific meaning of words helps us develop a more insightful grasp of ourselves and others.

Keep in mind, my focus here is to touch upon several topics that have been useful to my healing journey. Many books are dedicated to those subjects, and so I advise you to delve in with further reading on whatever areas of study spark your interest.

I don't delve into great detail about the actual events I am presenting because that's not the kind of book this is. My purpose here is about expressing the way I felt during and following these experiences. I understand a good deal more about human behavior than I did when these events occurred, and I no longer live in a place of blame, shame, guilt, or anger. I understand that humans can be assholes sometimes, myself included. I have forgiven myself and others for what took place. What I share within these pages comes from a place of love and gratitude, and that includes for the bad stuff that "happened to me" as well as the bad stuff I've done.

So know this: So many amazing people are out there holding on to unnecessary pain that causes suffering. This self-inflicted suffering leads to intrinsic unhappiness, which leads to mental, emotional, and physical ailments. Yes, we humans have the power to make ourselves physically sick, and unfortunately, it happens more often than we might expect. Our inner critic can be cruel and debilitating to our body. While anxiety is a necessary feeling to help us get out of undesirable situations and is something we all have, anxiety itself can be addictive. It can take over our lives if we allow it. Once anxiety does take over, it's extremely hard to learn new skills and end the negative habitual behavior (addiction). However, it is far from impossible.

I have had anxiety issues most of my life. I developed full-on panic attacks as an adult, which led to years of medication. This led to additional diagnoses ("diag-non-sense" as they say in the memoir and movie *Girl, Interrupted*) and additional medications ... and additional suffering being layered on myself and those I love most. It became a vicious cycle, and one that I later came to realize was mostly self-inflicted abuse. This unfortunate situation created room for others to mistreat me. I was so tolerant of so many different levels of abuse being heaped on me that, a lot of the time, I didn't even realize I was being wronged. I learned the hard way that the more I love myself, the less bullshit I will tolerate from other people, including from people I love.

I am far from perfect. I have made mistakes in my life and I will make more. I have gained the perspective on my journey to know that we all make mistakes, and we all will make more. Yet these are just snapshots of our lives. It's when the bad days of our mistakes start to outweigh the good days that it becomes a problem and leads to suffering.

I am excited, anxious, and a bit terrified to share this book with the world. And I have learned what fear is: both a lie and a sign of growth. Fear is often a sign you are moving in the right direction. If the thing that triggers your fear weren't scary, if it were just easy, everyone would do it. I am here to tell you that nothing of lasting value is easy—at first ... until one day, it is. And the next day, you raise your standards once again and try something harder.

After one mountain is climbed, there is another behind it. The challenge will not be easy; that's why it's called a challenge. And facing the fear around the challenge can often be a challenge in itself. What makes it get easier as you go is that by surrounding yourself with the right support system, you do not allow fear, anxiety, and self-sabotage to take over or hold you back.

I don't know how to end this introduction ... so let's just begin.

1

Your Past Does Not Define Your Future

I have spent countless hours staring at my computer screen. Although I have loved writing all my life and wanted to publish a book since taking my first creative writing class in middle school, here I sit ... blank mind ... blank screen. A strong desire to use my passion for writing to share my other passions—psychology and self-improvement—has brought me to this point. I have gathered pages of notes, journal entries, and unpublished blog posts about my experiences, not to mention a plethora of training manuals on every topic I've planned for this book. How do I now put all of that on the page in a way that will be compelling and meaningful?

A voice in my head suggests I may be, in fact, wasting my time. Who am I to write a book? What do I have to say that hasn't already been said by another, more qualified, person? What if it fails? I respond to myself, *What if I don't fail? What if fulfilling a lifelong dream were, in itself, a success?* Amazing, yes, and perhaps scary as heck.

Finally, I settle in to meditate and just be still for a few minutes. Out of the stillness, Ernest Hemingway comes to mind. I know very little about him—except he was a celebrated writer who lived in Key West and liked cats. Later, I take a few minutes to browse information about him on the internet, and I learn that he happened to have been born in the same town as me, which I find pretty cool. But then, I run across the following sentence attributed to Ernest Hemingway, which could not be more to the point:

All you have to do is write one true sentence.

Write the truest sentence that you know.

So I am going to take his advice, and for me that means I am going to throw all my shit out there and just get it out of the way. Some may be surprised at what they read. Some triggered. Maybe some will be inspired. Many may find it boring or depressing, or just not care one way or the other. And that will be okay too.

So here goes ...

My name is Jennifer. I grew up in the Chicago suburbs, one of two children born to teenage parents. They divorced when I was in elementary school. My parents lacked the emotional intelligence to create a stable, happy home life or even carry out a stable co-parenting dynamic. Both were burdened by multiple addictions with which they struggled. My dad moved out of state shortly after the divorce and became nonexistent in our world. He would sporadically pop back into our lives but never stayed long. He did not pay child support, and he rarely even called us (no cell phones back then to make it any easier).

My mom was left working two jobs when she could find them, and at times she could not find even one. We were on state aid and moved nearly every school year. It all depended on where she could afford to live at any given time. Sometimes the three of us lived together, and other times with family, or separated, living wherever we could. Often, she had a roommate or two, or a boyfriend to help with the bills. Mostly, we lived in a full house with minimal privacy.

I attended eight different schools. Making friends and trusting people was a challenge. When we weren't squeezing in with family, we would live in a run-down trailer park or low-income housing. One of our houses was off a busy road in between a used car dealership and a lumber yard. Kids at school, the rich kids, often teased me because my clothes weren't from the Gap or Express, which I thought was a huge deal. In my mind, only rich people shopped at the mall. I had no clue there were designer clothes which were even more expensive than that. My mom would use clothing vouchers and food stamps, and I was always embarrassed. I was on the free-lunch program at school, deepening my sense of feeling inferior and shameful. My mom drove a rusty car with a loud muffler. Sometimes it didn't even start.

There was a lot of physical violence, an abundance of drugs and alcohol, and always so many people in our household. Mom's boyfriends/husbands overlapped each other, and they were not men of high value. My mother foolishly trusted these men, and as a result, I was sexually abused by one of her boyfriends as well as others she brought around me—even one of the babysitters. Feeling safe was rare. I often sought solace and comfort at my grandparents' house. Their home was quiet and felt safe, and later, I even found a way to live with them.

My childhood was spent living as an adult, when I should have been able to enjoy my time being a child. I took care of my little brother to the best of my ability, making our lunches, walking him to school or the bus stop. As latchkey kids, we spent a lot of time home without my mom.

High school felt like torture. I became rebellious and could not have cared less about my grades. I remember begging my mom to help me because of my intense suicidal thoughts and irrational acting out. Early freshman year, I lost my virginity. I really liked that boy, and I believed that his having sex with me meant that he liked me in return. Yes, I know better now. I didn't try drugs until after high school. However, I did steal and crash a couple of cars. That behavior quickly led to my spending thirty days in an adolescent psych unit freshman year.

My deepest thanks to the State of Illinois for covering that bill, enabling me to have that most amazing experience. I will never forget it, and I mean that in a good way, although I know what I went through may sound like the more excruciating scenes from Susanna Kaysen's book *Girl, Interrupted*. I go more into this later, but in those thirty days, I learned a lot about myself and about my caregivers. I walked in with a huge chip on my shoulder, thinking I was a victim, and I walked out having a far better understanding of my relationships. It was definitely a catalyst for my future love of psychology. I even made friends that I kept for years. I met so many beautiful souls during that time. I am a work in progress, as are we all, but my experience during that chapter in my life taught me so much and gave me a deep appreciation I still feel when I look in the mirror.

I used boys to fill in my voids of insecurity left over from my dad's abandonment of our family and from the sexual abuse perpetrated on me by other men. I wasn't overly promiscuous, however; it wasn't always about being physically sexual. I confused being the focus of male desire with having value. I am forever grateful to my grandfather, who stepped in and taught me a lot about how to act like a lady, using minimal makeup and modest clothing. Unfortunately, it took a while for some of those lessons to sink in.

By the end of sophomore year, I had mastered the art of truancy. I say *mastered* since I was rarely caught. And I never served a single day of Saturday detention because I managed to talk my way out of it every time it came up.

My first stepfather was returned to prison for violent crimes during my high school years. He was so violent that I was removed from my mother's custody by DCFS, the department of children and family services. I became a ward of the state and was placed in family foster care, where kids are legally placed with their own family members but as a foster child. We were still part of the system with an assigned social worker and regulations that must be followed. We were in and out of courtrooms in the hoods of Chicago. That was followed by my living in a girls' group home for my entire junior year. Eventually, I was able to move back to my grandparents' home for the final time.

My stay in the home in Schaumburg, Illinois, was another dark time in my life. But it was also a time for which I am grateful. No matter how screwed up my life was, I saw firsthand that there were kids who had it even worse. I am so thankful for two social workers, Paula and Martha, who brought me such comfort and security. They were so special to me that they both attended my wedding seven years later.

I always knew we were a dysfunctional family. But I also knew that I was not going to be living the rest of my life like that. And I would be damned if I were ever going to raise my own children that way. All through high school, I tried my best to be as functional as I could. I used my resources as much as possible, but I was spinning out of control. I couldn't find anyone to help me except for school counselors or court-appointed social workers and therapists. I felt incredibly alone and invisible.

By my senior year, I had some inkling that I could change my life. In fact, it was then that I wrote down my very first goal list and taped it to the last month of my wall calendar. Yet I was so overwhelmed just trying to figure out where to start that I gave up. I had no idea of looking to a model who could show me how to put such a life together. So, I said, "Fuck it," and went on autopilot. I dropped out of school and started working, trying to take care of myself ... just like my parents had done years before.

Trauma Is in the Eye of the Beholder

As children, we are 100 percent dependent on our parents to provide, protect, teach, and love us. Our caregivers and life experiences—the good, the bad, and the ugly—help mold us into who we are. We are taught what to eat and how, what religion to follow, the details of our family's traditions. We even adopt similar belief systems through our other caregivers and our general environment. By example, all these people teach us how to love and be loved—including how to love ourselves.

Whether what they model about these things is healthy or trauma-producing, they pass down to us the things that they had been taught as children from their parents. As a result, we all have toxic habits that we are quite capable of using to obtain our needs. We don't have to have come from serial killer or narcissistic cult families to have learned and adopted unhealthy skills that can create seriously dysfunctional behaviors.

My parents made some big mistakes, ones hurtful to their children. Yet I know they still loved my brother and me. They did not set out to hurt us in any way. They were doing simply what they had been taught to do, and it was all that they knew how to do. My mom had more than one side to her, as is true for all of us—humans are complex beings.

My mom did step up in my adulthood. She was there for the birth of my daughter, and eventually she moved to Florida to be closer to me and help with my children. However, when I was a child, she did not show up at a single school event for me. Whenever there was a holiday program, I would hitch a ride with friends, even while I was in elementary school. In third grade, I was left crying alone in my room one evening because she was "too tired" after work to attend our school open house. I was on the Pom-Pom Squad in middle school, and she did not come to one game to watch me perform.

I cannot speak to my mom's personal struggles and challenges. I know only what I saw and remember from a child's perspective, as well as some bits she later shared with me, adult to adult, that I will not share in this book. I will talk about my stories, my perspective, but I will not share anything about her personal life that she would not have told to a stranger. And I certainly do not know all her demons and traumas.

One thing I do know is that something in my mom changed after her third divorce and with the birth of her first grandchild. After years of living with so many men, she never lived with a man again. She never even had another serious relationship with a man. She apologized to me for the pain she had caused me over the years. And she focused on her grandchildren. It is my personal belief that when my mom became a grandma, she was able to start healing herself. She made real changes in her life.

We are not all good or all bad—that is my belief. My mom was such a loving and giving person. She evolved, and in the last decade of her life, she was pretty remarkable. She became the grandmother my children deserved and adored. She also became the mother I had always wanted. She had made so many mistakes in her life, and a lot of them hurt me. But on the other hand, they made me who I am today, and I love that. My experiences made me a better mom. For one thing, I show up to nearly all my children's school activities. I am the mom I am today because of the mom my mother was not to me.

Trauma: *a deeply distressing or disturbing experience*

Trauma is in the eye of the beholder. It ranges from the results of severe physical, sexual, and mental abuse to a typical sibling rivalry or even being bullied. It can result from a caregiver invalidating our emotions or minimizing the impact of our trauma. Any negative event in our lives that we do not process properly can be a cause for traumatic scars. How we choose to deal (or not) with our traumas helps mold us too.

All parents make mistakes. Sometimes our parents' transgressions are small and can build grit, character, and resilience within us. Their effects on us can teach us how to properly take responsibility and make repairs for our own human errors. Sometimes, however, those mistakes can be catastrophic, resulting in extreme internal pain and unseen damage that needs attention and healing far into adulthood.

No matter what the mistake, more times than not, parents are not intentionally trying to hurt their children. They just don't know what they don't know. Often, while they may be fumbling in their efforts, they are doing the best they can, even if we can't see it and don't believe it.

No matter what happened to us growing up, it was beyond our control. We are not responsible for how our parents chose to raise us. But what we are responsible for—as adults—is our own personal growth and healing. We have a choice: find the lesson or find the excuse.

As we become adults, we make our own mistakes, which are often piggybacked on the mistakes of our parents. Nonetheless, it is still our responsibility to learn and heal from those mistakes as we continue our personal journey. Some children face situations of horrific abuse that can lead to lifelong trauma. Apart from such cases, for the most part, how we live our life as an adult human being is nobody's responsibility but our own. We have a choice. We can either follow in the footsteps of our parents and continue familial cycles of behaviors, or we can learn from their mistakes. We can choose to break those cycles for good and not teach them to our children.

Emotional Intelligence

Some people might say they are an alcoholic because they were raised by one. Others say they choose not to drink because they were raised by an alcoholic.

Self-awareness is a quality we all can learn. We each have so much internal power to create our own intrinsic happiness. It starts with acknowledging our strengths and weaknesses—healing our past and owning our mistakes. We have the ability to manage our thoughts, emotions, and behaviors. Although this process is not easy, it is a skill that can be developed. Just like a muscle, the more you exercise this new skill, the stronger it becomes.

You have probably heard the term *EQ* (*emotional intelligence quotient*). Yet you may not know exactly what is meant by that. Many people do not, and yet a high EQ can be more useful and empowering than even the highest of IQs (intelligence quotients). The person with the highest IQ is not always the one who is the most successful ... or the most happy. EQ is something also learned from our experiences or our environment. Not the case for IQ.

To clarify what emotional intelligence is, I will use the definition according to www.helpguide.org, which articulates it perfectly:

Emotional intelligence: *the ability to understand, use, and manage your own emotions in positive ways to relieve stress, communicate effectively, empathize with others, overcome challenges and defuse conflict ... helps you build stronger relationships, succeed at school and work, and achieve your career and personal goals ... to connect with your feelings, turn intention into action, and make informed decisions about what matters most to you.*

Emotional intelligence has multiple sides to it. We may well know what needs to be done in a given situation. And yet, what we would advise others to do is often different than what we ourselves actually do. EQ reflects different skill sets that enable one to accept criticism and personal responsibility. It means being able to say no when you need or want to say no, without feeling guilty. It is about having those uncomfortable conversations with loved ones, friends, and coworkers with compassion and without judgment. It's especially important when we are under pressure during difficult times, such as when we are dealing with death, job loss, or divorce. EQ balances having empathy for others with feeling compassion and love for ourselves.

If a child is raised in a household rife with poor communication and toxic fighting, chances are that child is going to adopt those same behaviors, until they choose to do otherwise. Yes, *choose.* We can learn new skills to raise our EQ and become more mindful of emotions, behaviors, and thoughts. We can learn new coping skills—basic, yet powerful skills. For example, labeling our emotions for starters, and then graduating to larger skills like setting boundaries for healthy and mature communication—and upholding them. I had a friend tell me once (after what I thought was our first fight), that she'd been mad at me several times without telling me. This behavior indicates a low-level EQ skill.

Our "Master Program"

Our subconscious mind controls most of what we do—90 to 99 percent of it. It is pretty much automatic. Think of your subconscious as a computer with unlimited memory that saves every single event in your life, including your birth. Most people are unaware the operation of their subconscious mind is so all encompassing.

According to bestselling author Brian Tracy:

> Your conscious mind is your objective or thinking mind. It has no memory, and it can only hold one thought at a time ... The function of your subconscious mind is to store and retrieve data. Its job is to ensure that you respond exactly the way you are programmed. Your subconscious mind makes everything you say and do fit a pattern consistent with your self-concept. This is your "Master Program."[1]

All our habits are managed by our subconscious mind. How we react to everything we experience, from biting our nails to worrying obsessively to driving our regular route to work to responding calmly in an emergency is controlled by our subconscious mind. It will do everything in its power to keep us safe. Safety, *as our subconscious understands the feeling*, is its primary aim. That may or may not be in our best interest because the yardstick by which it measures our safety is *familiarity*. It makes us comfortable so we won't want to change things. It has our comfort zones memorized. Our subconscious mind is designed

---

1. Briantracy.com

to protect us and can be challenging to reprogram. Nonetheless, it can be done.

Alerts from our subconscious mind are messages that trigger our reactions and responses, both emotionally and physically. These alerts warn of potential danger, pain, or discomfort, and if we fail to learn to control them, they will control us, possibly causing us even more pain. We are typically unaware of our subconscious habits, unaware of the stories we tell ourselves, of our limiting beliefs that are prohibiting personal growth and happiness.

Self-awareness, a decision to act, and new behaviors—these are what can enable us to slowly begin reprogramming our subconscious mind and create the peaceful life we desire. Our conscious mind has the ability to make commands (not demands) to the subconscious mind. At a safe pace, with a consistent amount of patience and self-compassion, we can end patterns and habits that are negatively impacting our lives and replace them with new habits—ones that are in alignment with our intrinsic happiness and self-worth.

Our Attachment Style

Another aspect of our upbringing that has ongoing impact in our adult relationships relates to what is called our *attachment style*, a theory developed in the 1950s by psychoanalyst John Bowlby, and later on, with psychoanalyst Mary Ainsworth. An individual's attachment style is developed and shaped in early childhood in response to the actions of the caregivers. There are four main adult attachment styles:

- **Secure**—autonomous
- **Dismissive Avoidant**—dismissing
- **Anxious**—preoccupied
- **Fearful/Disorganized**—unresolved

The last three of these styles are forms of insecure attachment. Each style uses its own way of dealing with close relationships and bonds. Mostly, all four are focused on long-term relationships, romantic relationships, and the parent-child relationship. As with most things, these run on a spectrum, and all of us at one time or another can experience different attachments. However, we do tend to have one primary attachment style. Half the population has a secure attachment style. That means the other half has insecure attachments, and this causes an interesting dance between individuals.

Secure: Low on avoidance, low on anxiety. Securely attached people are comfortable with intimacy, including emotional intimacy. They do not fear abandonment or rejection from their partners because as they were growing up, typically, their caregivers were consistent with how they raised them.

Dismissive Avoidant: High on avoidance, low on anxiety. These people are uncomfortable with closeness and primarily value independence and freedom. They are not worried about a partner's availability, and often push others away to avoid the possibility of getting hurt. This can stem from caregivers having been more neglectful than responsive, leaving the child to self-soothe and depend on themself.

Anxious: Low on avoidance, high on anxiety. These individuals crave closeness and intimacy and are very insecure about their relationship. They fear abandonment and intimacy despite the strong desire. This attachment style often stems from inconsistency shown by caregivers. Sometimes, they may have been present and responsive to the child's needs, while other times, not so much, causing confusion and anxiety.

Fearful/Disorganized: High on avoidance, high on anxiety. These people are uncomfortable with intimacy, especially emotional intimacy. They are worried about their partner's commitment and love. They can fluctuate between being dismissive and anxious. It stems from inconsistent behavior shown by caregivers, and possibly from having multiple caregivers with different styles.

We're only as needy as our unmet needs.

John Bowlby

A securely attached child will store an internal working model of a responsive, loving, reliable caregiver and of a self that is worthy of love and attention, and will bring these assumptions to bear on all other relationships. Conversely, an insecurely attached child may view the world as a dangerous place, in which other people are to be treated with great caution, and see himself as ineffective and unworthy of love.

Jeremy Holmes

If we have an insecure attachment style, this does not mean necessarily that our caretakers were abusive or intentionally negligent, although some are. A parent may overlook simple things in day to day life, perhaps paying too much attention to an electronic device and too little to a child's bid for attention. Or on the flip side, a parent may pay too much attention to the child, creating an unhealthy codependency that leads to an insecure attachment style because the child is never taught to self-soothe and become independent. Or maybe the parent is always telling the child to *just let things go* when difficult emotions arise. A parent who works or travels a lot may just not be there enough. And some parents justify not attending important events and experiences at their children's school by being "too tired" every time they're called upon to show up.

These things hurt. Such behaviors are not abusive. Yet while their negative impact is unintentional, they still cause a child a lot of emotional pain. The result can be development in the child of an attachment style that is anxious, fearful, or dismissive, producing a lot of pain and confusion in their adult relationships.

Our attachment style is *something we have the power to alter*, enabling us to become more securely attached. It is part of our past and an example of what we have the power to change. Nonetheless, it is subconscious behavior, and changing our attachment style hinges on self-awareness, topics we will cover in this book.

If you have a secure attachment, congratulations. Your battle during this lifetime typically is less torturous than for those of us with insecure attachments. But even securely attached people have shit to deal with. I recommend reading more about this theory and learning your attachment style through research and quizzes. You may also want to check out my website for resources at www.jenslifecoaching.com.

I Define Me

Today, I am a happily divorced mother of three, a certified life coach and a health coach, author, and blogger. My childhood was beyond my control. Everything after the time I attained the age of eighteen years has been and remains not only within my control, but also my responsibility. To be a victim of my childhood circumstances and past experiences or to rise up because of them—these are my choices. Making the right choice as an adult is my responsibility.

For many years, I created and carried inside me a recurring nightmare. By suppressing and repressing my inner demons and hiding from my traumas for most of my life, I was haunted by my past. And what my memory ignored, my body remembered all too well, causing confusion and pain.

As a consequence, I hated my mother. I carried that hatred inside for years. I resented all her mistakes that had made my childhood hell and shadowed my adult life. I blamed her for not teaching me how to have a healthy relationship with myself and others, which I believed led to my divorce. Angry and miserable, I maintained limited boundaries for myself and let people walk all over me, even as I continued to not understand why this kept happening to me.

Repression is done subconsciously. Our minds have the power to "erase" conscious memories with the intention of protecting us. Unfortunately, our subconscious mind isn't all that intelligent because, in its drive to keep us safe, it often does more harm than good. We may not understand our demons and fears, all while acting in a way that we don't want to because we don't remember why we feel compelled to do so. We remain haunted.

Suppression is a conscious choice. We may intentionally avoid certain memories, feelings, or situations for many reasons. We still remember them, but we can disassociate and block them. Whether we suppress or repress this knowledge, we are haunted.

***Resentment**: a feeling of indignant displeasure or persistent ill will at something regarded as a wrong, insult, or injury*

—Merriam-Webster

In spite of my persistent anger and unhealthy relationships, I was determined to find intrinsic happiness and a way to heal. I read book after book on personal development, relationships, and trust. I took classes, hired coaches, and used multiple types of therapies to finally put it all together. It is now my life's purpose to help others find their intrinsic happiness.

As an adult, I have made many mistakes, some of which I share and own in this book. I have lied, cheated, and caused problems for myself and for others, and sometimes, it was done unintentionally. For nearly a decade, I was misdiagnosed and treated for bipolar disorder. None of these things define me. Most people do not even know these things about me. These are my experiences, my struggles, and they have helped mold me into the person I am today. Each day is simply a snapshot of who I truly am.

And I happen to love myself today. Let's be real. Every single person on this planet has done a thing or two ... or a hundred ... that they are not proud of. Unfortunately, not everyone takes responsibility and learns the valuable lessons waiting behind the mistakes. We are rarely 100 percent victim in our adult experiences, and we must take responsibility for our actions.

I have qualities of which I am proud, qualities that may not even have existed had I not survived certain traumas and experiences. I am far from perfect, and I guarantee that I will make plenty more mistakes simply because I am human. But I no longer choose to be a victim. Shit happens to all of us, leaving us no excuses. Instead, we get to own our adult lives with the freedom to choose to live the happiest possible version of ourselves.

It may have taken twenty-plus years of trial and error, therapy, and self-development, but I finally figured out intrinsic happiness. And I cannot wait to share it with you in an easy-to-understand way. My life has been filled with such joy as I work with my individual clients and witness each of them step into their power.

> *I am not what happened to me; I am what I choose to become.*
>
> Carl Jung

2

Your Subconscious Mind at Work

Watch your thoughts, for they become your words.
Watch your words, for they become your actions.
Watch your actions, for they become your habits.
Watch your habits, for they become your character.
Watch your character, for it becomes your destiny.

Anonymous

When I shared the story of my writer's block in the previous chapter, I summarized what took place over a period of weeks for the sake of keeping it simple. But the point is that my writer's block was a matter of my subconscious mind at work, and I'll get back to that shortly. But first, here are some things to think about regarding the operation of the subconscious mind.

According to Brian Tracy, whom you met in chapter one, "The function of your subconscious mind is to store and retrieve data."[1] And here is a general definition of subconscious mind.

1. Briantracy.com

Subconscious: *the part of your mind that notices and remembers information when you are not actively trying to do so, and influences your behavior even though you do not realize it*

—Cambridge Dictionary

According to the pain pleasure principle of Sigmund Freud, one of the founding fathers of psychology, humans have a need to avoid pain and to gain pleasure. Therefore, our conscious mind reviews data from our subconscious mind to find and repeat ways to do just that.

Now, to make it even trickier, the subconscious mind doesn't really like change too much, not even positive change. It's programmed to keep us safe. Any sort of change or new habit has the potential to be painful, and the subconscious mind wants to protect us by avoiding that uncertainty. Depending on our individualized programming, it will use all our own tricks and old habits against us, self-sabotaging in order to stay in the same familiar routine. These tricks and habits can become *defense mechanisms.*

Defense mechanism: *an often unconscious mental process (such as repression) that makes possible compromise solutions to personal problems*

—Merriam-Webster

We find these "solutions" quite useful and effective in everyday life to avoid conscious conflict, anxiety, and pain. Even if our routine is harmful for us or perhaps slowly killing us, such as smoking cigarettes or staying in a toxic environment or relationship, we will find reasons to not make those changes. We each have our own set of defense mechanisms we've adopted or have been taught. Examples are substance dependency, codependency, denial, and projection, to name a few. It takes a strong, consistent conscious effort to make any changes.

We may *justify* or *rationalize* (two more defense mechanisms) staying at a job that causes too much stress because "the money is good." This is just an excuse so we can tell ourselves we don't have any other choice, when in reality we do. However, the other choice is more challenging, so we stay where it's easier. We may justify staying in a toxic relationship "for the kids," when in reality, we remain in place out of fear of being alone or lack of self-worth. We do this because our "data," securely stored within our subconscious mind, has been programmed to keep us alive and safe by keeping up in our comfort zone.

Familiar = Safe
Safe = No Additional Pain

Unfortunately, we all have pain in our lives, and bad shit happens to all of us. People break up and divorce. People lose their jobs. If we are lucky, we get to grow old. People die. And let's not forget the wrath of Mother Nature as she tears apart homes and businesses with her fierce tornadoes, hurricanes, and other "Acts of God." And unfortunately ...

Pain + Resistance = Suffering

Our minds are so powerful that they can even create incurable defense mechanisms such as *narcissistic personality disorder*, a condition characterized by an exaggerated sense of self-importance and lack of empathy, which can stem from severe childhood trauma and neglect. A mind can even create physical ailments such as migraines, ulcers, or even cancer.[2] Simply believing we are going to get sick can actually make it happen.

Another interesting fact about our subconscious programming is that it understands only the present moment. Meaning, it does not understand what has already happened or what has not yet happened. If we are thinking about an event, then our subconscious mind thinks it is happening right now, which is why when we think of a lemon, often our mouths water. Or when we think of a past painful memory or watch a sad movie, we may cry. A smell or a song can trigger a forgotten memory. It's also why a subconscious mind responds to positive affirmations, or as motivation expert Tony Robbins suggests, *incantations in the now*, such as "I am amazing" instead of "I will be amazing."

2. Joseph Murphy, *The Power of your Subconscious Mind*. (Soho Books, 2010)

So, what does my writer's block have to do with it? We all have our own internal belief system and defense system that we have adopted so far in our lifetime—from our parents, environment, friends, spouses, peers, TV, and a host of other influences. We agree to a belief system—true and false—and we aren't even aware of it. And just like for every other person out there, some of those beliefs will limit your potential growth and happiness; hence the reason it's called a "limiting" belief.

Limiting Beliefs

A *limiting belief* is a belief about yourself or state of mind that restricts you in some way. We all have limiting beliefs or stories we tell ourselves that help us generate justifications (excuses) to not do something.

I never realized some of my limiting beliefs until they were pointed out to me by one of my coaches. My bipolar label, for example, was an unhealthy defense mechanism that I was able to hide behind while continuing my habits born of anxiety, depression, and self-loathing. We are what we believe. The old me believed I was "crazy" and unstable, so I often acted that way. To this day, all my coaches keep me on point and on guard against any limiting beliefs they hear coming from me.

Remember what the subconscious mind does: it stores and retrieves data. The conscious mind collects the data and has the ability to change the data it stores. Once the new "data," or new behavior, becomes more and more consistent, it becomes a new habit and is followed by a new identity. A new program is now installed into the database.

The most effective way to change our behavior is through taking baby steps that create momentum toward bigger changes.

Some of my old limiting beliefs included the sense that I was not intelligent. I believed that because so often I had been told I wasn't smart. I also believed, in spite of my lifelong desire to write, that I was not a good writer. Therefore, I could not have anything valuable to share, and trying to do so meant I would be embarrassed and ashamed yet again. A current limiting belief I am dealing with involves perfectionism. Part of my "writer's block" keeps telling me if I don't turn in 3,400 words of perfection to my publisher the very first time, then I suck at writing and I am wasting everyone's time—once again reinforcing negative self-beliefs I harbor.

Obviously, fact one is that neither of those beliefs is true. Fact two is that I no longer believe either of them. Notice how those contradictory statements about beliefs represent two different facts because perception is reality, whether the thing perceived is true or not. The truth is I am intelligent, and I have the IQ results to prove it. And this book is worth writing and is valuable to many people. Here, I remind myself that even Stephen King doesn't turn in a perfect first draft.

I consciously tell myself that no matter what I write, good or bad, the seven billion humans on this planet will never 100 percent agree on anything, let alone all of them finding my book valuable. I remind myself that there may be haters who will always have negative beliefs about me and my writing, and that's okay. The truth is, I don't like everyone myself.

Anyway, just because I do not believe these things any longer doesn't mean their presence is completely erased from the database of my subconscious mind. So, to avoid potential pain (writing a shitty book followed by shame and embarrassment), I subconsciously scan for previous habits that have worked for me in the past to justify procrastination via writer's block. I naturally resort to old beliefs and redirect my attention toward something else I am more confident doing. So I use the time I had set aside for writing to work on my coaching business ... or continue my education ... or work in my workshop ... or, one of my all-time favorites, clean or organize anything I can find.

To get over that internal fear and the resulting blockade of my limiting beliefs and just write, I had to consciously choose to do something different—just start typing. Oh ... and did I mention that I struggle with perfectionism? Which leads to procrastination, causing a vicious cycle of self-sabotage.

Discomfort = Growth

Life Beyond the "Crazy"

Praying is when we talk to God, while meditation is when we listen.

Edgar Cayce

I pray and talk to God daily, as many people do, and I have done so most of my life. Meditation and being mindful of my thoughts are skills I developed over the last several years, and they've turned out to be quite powerful. Sitting still and listening led me to Ernest Hemingway's quote in chapter one. It was enough motivation for me to create enough pleasure to actually start transferring my notes and outlines into the damn chapter ... even knowing haters may well hate this book, no matter how brilliant it may or may not be. And knowing that those who love me and believe in me will support me either way. And it gives me pleasure knowing that my mom would have loved it, no matter what.

I chose to simply start the chapter instead of not writing it at all because the pleasure outweighed the pain in that moment. Two weeks later, I had almost 2,000 words (1,828, to be exact), with zero time spent on grammar or any sort of editing. I had two choices: (1) procrastinate further, aiming for immediate perfection and not turn anything in, which would lead to internal shame and guilt, or (2) turn in what I had and be proud that I was turning in draft one of my first chapter of my first book. When we celebrate even the small things, we are able to truly appreciate all things which lead to bigger celebrations.

We all have a subconscious mind, a memory bank of everything we've ever seen, heard, or felt. Every face we've seen, every smell we ever inhaled, every experience we felt. It remembers every choice we consciously made and has created a pattern or a set of habits to get what we want, need, and desire.

As babies, we learn that when we cry, we either consistently receive the attention we seek or we do not. Even if our caregivers are consistent in caring for us, this response in itself can lead to other behaviors—some positive, some negative. Potentially unhealthy defense mechanisms may form to ensure we receive our desired needs. A parent who reliably gives in to whiny behavior or tantrums indirectly teaches the child a skill for getting needs met. These behaviors, when continually rewarded, can lead to formation of habits. Such habits create our beliefs and our identity, and sometimes, they become detrimental to our lives. These habits, for better or worse, also help create our initial attachment style.

Shortly after my daughter was born in 2010, I was diagnosed with bipolar disorder. Let me rephrase that: I was *misdiagnosed* with bipolar disorder by a psychiatrist and then highly medicated for years to follow. At the time, my oldest was seven and my second child was just a few months old. I had to wean my daughter from breastfeeding before starting the medication the psychiatrist prescribed, and it broke my heart. She was the only baby I had been able to actually nurse successfully, and having to stop nursing her caused more depression in me. I confused "being educated" with "having intelligence" and trusted my doctor.

I was dealing with postpartum depression, and my marriage was on the brink of divorce for reasons outside the scope of this book. I was battling two double-breast infections AND continuing to breastfeed my newborn, all while sleeping in my son's bedroom away from my husband. I was emotionally unstable, and my thoughts and actions demonstrated as much. I had zero family support nearby, and being an introvert, I didn't have a lot of friends that I opened up to. I felt so alone and isolated ... and "crazy." I was filled with anxiety, and having the bipolar label provided me with a new defense mechanism. I forced down more pills, and I focused solely on my children ... neglecting myself more and more each day.

Fast-forward four years ... baby number three is less than a year old. My marriage is still struggling, and I am now on 1200 mg of lithium a day ... a different "antipsychotic" drug.

Can you believe that's what they are actually called? Antipsychotic drugs? Like the word *psychotic* didn't add enough additional shame to my "brokenness." Yet I was still miserable and still acting unstable more days that not. On top of my unstable mind, I was internally battling my hatred and anger for my mother, who had since moved closer to us—*at my request*. As much as I loved that woman, my pregnancy hormones tended to bring out repressed feelings and undealt-with trauma from my past. I had a love/hate inner battle going with her. I wanted her near me.

I wanted my children around her because she was amazing with them. Yet parts of me still deeply resented the mistakes she had made when I was a child.

Something has got to change, I thought. So, I started intensive psychotherapy because now I had come to believe that, in addition to bipolar disorder, I also had *borderline personality disorder* (BPD) and that must be the reason the medication wasn't helping stabilize my emotions and state of mind. I had self-diagnosed this additional condition, defined in part by Merriam-Webster's Dictionary as "marked by unstable, intense emotions and mood with symptoms, including instability in interpersonal relationships and self image." I came to this conclusion after the idea was planted in my head by my spouse.

That's why I started *dialectical behavior therapy* (*DBT*), a form of cognitive therapy that helps us see both sides of a situation, balancing our emotions and logic. The therapist I started dialectical behavior therapy with is the one who told me I did not have either disorder. I didn't believe her. I told her she didn't see me at home.

I was spending five hours a week between individual and group therapy. Only my husband knew this because I was ashamed of and embarrassed about my "crazy." I was dissecting my life and peeling back layer after layer of all my past and present traumatic experiences, trying to heal and be less *crazy*. A few months in, my therapist at the time, who specialized in BPD and was treating me with dialectical behavior therapy, said, "Jen, you are not bipolar and you do not have borderline personality disorder. You just haven't learned to deal with your thoughts and emotions properly, and you lack proper skills."

I was thrilled to hear those words. When I shared that information with my husband, whom I loved and admired at the time, he curtly interrupted with, "If you aren't bipolar, then what's wrong with us?" I immediately felt crushed and defeated. I wondered the same thing.

So I denied the truth of what my therapist had told me. I continued on with therapy and medications, doubling down on the belief that I was indeed bipolar with borderline personality disorder. And I continued to think and act the part. I took on all the blame for the problems in our lives, and I tried so hard to be a better wife and person. We had tried marriage counseling off and on over the years but had never done anything consistent. After I started to work on myself, I was noticing positive personal changes, and yet, it became clear the marriage still was not getting better—at all. Oddly, it was getting worse.

Over the next couple of years, I sought out several types of treatment and therapy. I was determined to find something to make me sane and happy. I wanted to not be so angry all the time, especially toward my mom. I loved her so much, but I just couldn't figure out how to forgive her. I wanted so badly to just let go of my resentment of her hurtful mistakes. Finally figuring out all of that required that I go within myself.

I consulted with multiple top psychologists in my area and other specialists on mental health disorders—all in all, a total of nine. And every single one of them received the same intake answers, only to tell me the same thing ... *You are not bipolar and you do not have borderline personality disorder*. They all told me they believed that it was my toxic marriage and family environment that was triggering these behaviors.

The only doctor who disagreed was the doctor who had been prescribing me medications and seeing me every thirty to ninety days for a fifteen-minute medication evaluation. He even told me specifically, after I suggested that I may not be bipolar, "I have twelve years of education and the PhD for a reason. I am certain you have bipolar, and you should just let that seed die."

I had continued seeing this prescribing doctor for about seven years. I didn't start getting second opinions until after I had left my husband, and my life coach helped me get over that fear. I asked the original doctor about the possibility I had been misdiagnosed probably six to twelve months prior to finding a new doctor, but he remained adamant he was correct.

The power of our subconscious mind is extraordinary and mind blowing. Letting go of the label of bipolar was painful for me because I had no answer to this conundrum: *If I am not bipolar, why am I acting so unstable?* At least if I were bipolar or had BPD, then I would have had an excuse for my "crazy" and a reason for subconsciously enabling my behaviors. Before I could release myself from reliance on this label to explain why I acted in the ways I did, I first had to accept that my failed marriage was not all my fault. That was why I couldn't fix it. I had to come to terms with the likelihood that my marriage was never going to improve.

Addictions aren't always tangible, like smoking, drinking, food or substance abuse, or gambling. Many of us do not realize that our minds can be addicted to almost *anything*—a negative or positive mindset or inner dialogue. Even behaviors such as over-worrying (causing anxiety), lying, sidestepping our problems, or living in the past filled with regrets have the potential to become addictive. Some internal addictions can become toxic and hurtful both to ourselves and those around us.

Skills for Healing

Whether you think you can or you think you can't, you are right.

Henry Ford

When I was younger, I was not taught how to deal with emotions and intense situations properly. I was taught to "just let it go." If something was bothering us, we didn't talk it out because that could possibly lead to a fight, and in our family, fighting was "bad." Although the intention of the adults promoting this approach was well-meaning, by engaging in that unhealthy behavior (defense mechanism), we found ourselves steeped in unresolved anxiety, anger, and resentment. These are low EQ skills.

Suppressing our negative feelings created poor communication skills, which also trickled into our other relationships, even our school and work environments. Of course, this dysfunctional approach to dealing with conflict led to the inevitable ... resentment and fighting. The simmering emotions and anger we'd consciously suppressed (another defense mechanism) were left bottled up inside us, sometimes for years. The mounting pressure would end up leading to an explosive fight at some point, instead of a healthy argument that could have been resolved much sooner by using more appropriate skills.

It is absolutely impossible to go through life without being upset with others. Disagreements are part of life. The disagreement or fight in itself is not the problem. When toxicity arises, it is not caused by the argument, but the way it is handled and resolved, and in how relationships are repaired afterward, or not. It's true, we all have an ego, and that can get in our way of handling conflicts that arise in our day to day lives. (Even Mahatma Gandhi had an ego.) But by having an adult conversation and putting our egos aside, this creates a high EQ skill.

Ego: *the part of you that is engaged in self-justification. There are at least two interrelated parts of the ego. One part ... enables self-reflective awareness and the capacity to justify one's actions to self and others. ... strong motivational forces are in operation as the ego generates defenses ... to maintain a justifiable place in the world.*

—Gregg Henriques, PhD[3]

Nearly two decades ago, a family member had just moved into a new home, and most of the family was involved in the moving-in process. My job was to watch the little ones. As I entered the home and greeted everyone, a family friend was in the backyard doing serious manual labor. As I stood on the upstairs porch, this family friend shouted hello to me from across the yard and accidentally called me by the name of another female in my family. I took absolutely no offense at this mistake, as I have known this woman for years and knew she was just tongue-tied. I proceeded to call out my hello back to her, reminding her that wasn't my name as I laughed with her.

Twenty feet behind me, inside the house, another member of my family overheard ONLY my part of the conversation. She took offense to my saying I wasn't this person and assumed I was making a jab at that person for not being present to help with the work. She didn't ask any questions but proceeded to gossip about her perception of what I'd said. As a result, a mini-clique within my family harbored ill feelings toward me. Several years later, this incident was brought to my attention for the first time. This is an example of low EQ and poor communication skills.

As an adult, I was still not dealing with my emotions and certain situations or relationships in a healthy manner, which led me down a

3. Henriques, Gregg, PhD. "What Is the Ego?" *Psychology Today*, (May 28, 2021)

path of self-destruction. My thoughts became more and more negative and self-loathing. I believed every critical word spoken to me from others who talked down to me, causing me to believe I was worthless and brainless. I was filled with shame and embarrassment and insecure about my sexuality. The trauma of the sexual abuse I had endured, as well as my father's abandoning us, the actions and inactions of my toxic mother, and my own eventually toxic marriage—all had come together to affect every aspect of my understanding of who I was.

I had no boundaries; heck, I didn't know what a boundary was. I didn't have any communication skills, let alone skills for conflict resolution. And I sure didn't understand human behavior one bit. I lacked awareness, both about myself and those around me. I was always seeking validation from others for the few strengths I felt I did have, and I attached the label of bipolar to explain and justify why my marriage was failing. I found myself walking a downward sloping path, drawn by my feelings of utter worthlessness. I ended up having an affair, and I was miserable. I was in so much pain it felt as if I were dying from the combined effects of sustaining a million papercuts.

One time, we had company over for a barbecue. I was in the kitchen prepping the meat and doing all the side dishes while my then-husband handled the actual grilling part. One of the guests who was helping asked me how to turn our grill on, and I told her I had no clue because I had never grilled anything. She was so condescending and shitty as she criticized me for not knowing something so "easy," all the time laughing. I remember feeling quite angry at her for her unnecessary commentary. And at the same time, I felt ignored and invalidated for all the stuff I did know.

Looking back, I feel sad for the woman. I now know that she was reflecting what was inside her. She must have been unhappy and feeling herself to be unintelligent, putting me down in order to feel superior. Having become fully aware of and secure in my intelligence level, as well as my EQ, I am pretty much immunized to that kind of toxicity.

But back then, the only thing I felt decent at was being "just a stay-at-home mom," the perfect "Stepford wife." I didn't realize that people who would gratuitously criticize and attempt to diminish me were only projecting their internal poison onto me. And so, in turn, I amplified the effects of their negative behavior by projecting that poison onto myself. I felt uncomfortable in my own skin, and I found myself becoming more and more reclusive. And the day came when I decided I had had enough!

It was during the aftermath of Hurricane Irma, a powerful storm that caused widespread damage. My husband came home drunk after work. We'd been having repeated fights about this behavior that entire year. Now, here we were—at home with no power and a generator we could use for only one room in our house. He was supposed to have met me and his family for dinner, and he "forgot." I moved out six weeks later because I finally came to terms with the fact that he was never going to change. And I knew that something had to change.

I prayed differently this time. I asked for strength to make a life-altering decision. Shortly after that, as I sat still and aware of my thoughts, I found the courage to change my surroundings, and I left my husband.

It wasn't until I was working with my first life coach, Alma, that I realized I had been using *bipolar* as a label to define myself. Here I was creating a happier life for myself and no longer thinking or acting as unstable as I once had, but still ingesting lithium and enduring all of its uncomfortable side effects. Finally, I built up the courage to believe the doctors and accept that I wasn't bipolar. Guided by my psychologist, I found a new doctor to work with, and soon after, I weaned myself off all medications.

That was in 2019. Today, I am the most stable and the happiest I have ever been in my entire life. Those who didn't know me before find it hard to believe that I ever felt so lowly about myself and could act that way. They find it especially hard to believe that I thought I wasn't smart. And those who know the new-and-improved Jen say things like, "Happiness looks gorgeous on you."

Baby Steps

You don't become what you want, you become what you believe.

Oprah Winfrey

One of the first and biggest changes I made was to my internal dialogue. And that, in turn, started to change my belief system. Our subconscious mind is like a garden, and our conscious mind plants seeds in the garden. And through repetition, those seeds bloom. Normally, when people ask us how we are, our automatic response is "fine" or "good." One day, I decided to not use those words any longer. When I am asked how I am, my new responses are "I'm awesome!" or "I'm fantastic!" or something similar. Subtle changes like that build momentum and create a new tide.

Habit change comes from taking baby steps, or "two-mm shifts," as Tony Robbins calls them. In order to change our identity, we have to work backward. First we change our behaviors, which leads to a change in our belief system, and finally to a change in our identity.

When I make a subtle change, perhaps simply by saying "I'm awesome!" and watching my tone of voice and smiling, I am not only causing a new alert in my own mind but am also causing myself to act differently, even if only slightly—and in a positive way. It also adds a spark to others because they are often expecting the usual "good" or "fine," and often my new response causes them to smile and respond differently too. It becomes a ripple effect, and the more I do it, the more I love it. Now my new baseline is raised. When I say I am *fine* or *good* ... that's generally when I am not so fine.

3

The Mental Health System Is Failing Us

Stigma*: a mark of disgrace associated with a particular circumstance, quality, or person*

Stigma is a very powerful and hurtful mechanism in the mental health world. Those who may have the intention to protect people from potential harm so often end up projecting wrongful judgments onto a person or situation, causing additional distress by stigmatizing them. It happens not only within the mental health system, but also within marriages, families, work environments, and even our judicial system.

Society acts as if mental health is only for the "crazy and dangerous." Sure, *Gone Girl* types and other varieties of sociopath are very real. From John Wayne Gacy, rapist and serial killer, to Elizabeth Holmes, who built a billion-dollar company on nothing but lies, they can turn up anywhere. But in fact, those personality disorders are rare. They may be what comes to mind since they boost news ratings, or characters like Hannibal Lector make for interesting movies.

According to statistics found on the National Alliance on Mental Illness website:[1]

1. https://www.nami.org/mhstats

- 1 in 5 U.S. adults experiences mental illness each year
- Suicide is the 2nd leading cause of death among people aged 10–14
- 1 in 6 U.S. youth aged 6–17 experiences a mental health disorder each year
- At least 8.4 million people in the U.S. provide care to an adult with a mental or emotional health issue

Overall, *anxiety* leads the way, followed by *depression*. Both conditions are common and treatable. On the flip side, both conditions, if left untreated, can lead to suicide. If you are one of the lucky ones who hasn't had personal experience on some level with the impact of these conditions, I'm sure you can still appreciate the tragic loss of Robin Williams and the mask he wore to cover up his inner struggles.

According to the Centers for Disease Control, suicide increased 33 percent during the period from 1999 to 2019. *Hmmm ... social media and online bullying, perhaps?* In 2019, an estimated 12 million adult Americans seriously thought about suicide.

Stigma causes unnecessary suffering to so many people in need of help. They hide their needs and live in fear, often as their mental health worsens. They don't want to be a burden to their loved ones, emotionally, physically, or financially. Then, if their mental health struggles do negatively impact their loved ones, they carry an additional burden. It becomes a seemingly impossible choice: hide their suffering and hope no one notices or reach out for help and risk burdening others with their problems. They fear being branded with a stigma that may be believed by others. Even worse, they begin to believe the stigma themselves.

Mental health disorders impact 44 percent of the LGBTQIA community. Could that be because they have several stigmas already projected onto them?

America is the wealthiest nation in the world. Yet it ranks as having one of the highest rates of suicide in the world annually. It comes in at fourteenth for happiness and satisfaction. More proof that money does not create happiness.

If we are so smart and hardworking, then why are we so blind? Why the hell aren't we bringing more awareness, understanding, and compassion to mental health? Maybe if we put our mental health first with better treatment plans, we'd be a happier society. Maybe we wouldn't be so angry with ourselves and each other.

Unfortunately, the stigma around mental health is a global issue. The leading cause of disability worldwide is depression.[2] Mental health awareness is something that needs to be brought to the forefront of humanity's concerns.

Just Let It Go ...

During my freshman year in high school, I spent thirty days locked in an adolescent psychiatric unit. I had been living with my grandparents, and I remember begging my family for help because I was so depressed, with rising suicidal thoughts. I had already started collecting my grandparents' pills, a little at a time, contemplating the deed. I was in such a dark place and really believed the pain would go away if I were to just die. I would cry when nobody was looking because if I cried in front of anyone, I was told things like "it's not that big of a deal" or "just let it go." What could a fifteen-year-old possibly have to deal with that is so difficult?

Hmmm ... you may have a better understanding of what so many teenagers have to deal with by the end of this book; at least you will know what I personally had to deal with. The only thing stopping me from ending my internal pain before I was finally admitted to the hospital was my own religious belief about suicide and my personal fear of hell.

During my stay, I was among many coed adolescents with issues similar to mine, and many with worse. It wasn't as intense as portrayed in the book and movie *Girl, Interrupted*, but it was scary sometimes. In order to exit the psych unit, we had to be escorted through two locked doors by a member of the medical team. I was on suicide watch for the first twenty-four hours and had to be observed by staff while I slept. I was so relieved when I got my first roommate, a freshman with bipolar

2. https://www.nami.org/mhstats

disorder. She was nice, and she had previous experience in this environment, so she made me feel a little safer. I think of her often.

Sex, alcohol, and drug abuse were some of the many forms of self-medication that we teens used. Some were medicated as prescribed by doctors. I remember wanting to be medicated like some of the other kids because then I would have a reason to explain my being a burden to myself and my family. Instead, during thirty days of twenty-four-hour evaluation, I entered a strict regime of intense therapies, including independent, group, and family therapy. I was never medicated—not once—and was explicitly told by the medical team that I did not have any manic-depressive disorders or personality disorders. I was just dealing poorly with personal trauma.

Toward the end of my stay, a new female patient was admitted. She had dissociative identity disorder (DID), or what was back then called multiple-personality disorder. I remember sitting in the recreational therapy room when I learned of her diagnosis upon meeting her. My immediate thought was, *She's really messed up*. Stigma? Judgment? We sat the rest of the time and talked, like normal teen girls. But later, when she changed personalities in front of me for the first time, I intuitively knew something really bad had happened to her that had created such a strong, protective self. That was the first time I became interested in psychology and the mind.

As I am typing all of this detail, so many memories of my experience there surface. I remember how my dad came to a family session. As I am thinking of that moment, it brings tears to my eyes. How much effort it had to have been for him to get to me! An unemployed alcoholic with a revoked driver's license living thirty miles from the hospital and having no established relationship with his suicidal daughter. That effort alone shows my dad loved me, even though he couldn't always show it. Clearly, he had his own pain and struggles that, although hurtful toward me, were in no way caused by me.

I was discharged after thirty days (that was all the insurance covered) without the need to attend daily outpatient care, unlike many of my inpatient roommates. I was advised to seek individual and family counseling so I could learn to deal with my dysfunctional family dynamics and past trauma. Unfortunately, that did not happen consistently enough, only leading to more trauma and mental health issues down the road.

In my early twenties, I developed social anxiety and generalized anxiety, which led to a deep depression. I started taking antianxiety and antidepressant medications—medications that I became dependent on for many years as I lived with the label of "I have anxiety and I get sad." Every single day, I was telling myself that same story while I unconsciously played the victim.

The Silence Is Deafening

"Children are resilient." That's what the experts say. I do not understand how any mental health professional who's ever flipped through the current *Diagnostic & Statistical Manual of Mental Disorders* (DSM-5) can say that with a straight face. Clearly, paying for all that textbook knowledge can only go so far. And this I know, because I know they are wrong.

Yes, children are resilient as they overcome separation anxiety from their caregivers because that helps mold them into functioning adults. They are resilient when they are mildly picked on by their siblings, as that creates thicker skin. They are resilient when learning how to properly deal with death and dying because it's a part of life nobody can avoid. Children are resilient when they are taught healthy ways to deal with negative emotions and the hurt inflicted by other people. They can become resilient through divorce or separation when parents put their differences aside and focus only on the well-being of the children.

Children are *not* resilient when they witness their parents constantly fighting or physically hurting each other. Children are not resilient when abandoned by a parent or when parents continuously weaponize the children against each other. They are not resilient after consistently watching their caregivers struggle with substance abuse. Children are not resilient when subjected to molestation, incest, or rape.

Certain traumas must be dealt with through proper therapy and healing. Until that happens, our traumas will haunt us. We can repress and suppress all we want. We can throw in some more unhealthy defense mechanisms like denial and pretend nothing happened. We can cry in private, yet act like we are okay. But just because the child (or adult) isn't talking about the pain they suffer doesn't mean they aren't thinking about it, even ruminating about it. It doesn't mean they aren't triggered in ways they do not understand, physically, emotionally, and mentally. Or that they aren't looking for a way to avoid it. Remember the subconscious mind? It likes to avoid pain and gain pleasure.

Avoiding the pain that my had father abandoned me and gaining the pleasure from boys being attracted to me, though I wasn't acting overly promiscuous, I certainly did like the attention. Another vicious cycle.

From my personal experiences with being sexually molested, I know for a fact how haunting those horrible traumas can be. It took me several months to tell my mom about the first molestation. Unfortunately, though, it was never spoken of again, and the perpetrator was permitted to continue hanging around. Later, I was molested by three additional men in our circle. I feared not being heard once again, and I kept this abuse a secret for years. I suppressed the trauma that ultimately haunted me for decades.

It was like it never happened. I repressed certain memories and suppressed those emotions of shame and guilt and disgust. I buried the wounds that would inevitably impact my life and relationships in such a negative way, especially around my capacity to feel sexual trust. It wasn't until I started intense therapy in my thirties that I really began to heal those wounds that have now become scars. Therapy wasn't easy or fun, but it was essential for my internal happiness and mental well-being. (More details to come.)

Between the ages of nine and thirteen, not only did I suffer molestation from four men, but I was raised in an unstable and inconsistent environment that developed my personal avoidant attachment style.

Before I get into this, let me remind you what an *attachment style* is with a quote from one of my favorite resources on this topic. Thais Gibson, founder of The Personal Development School and expert in attachment style, puts it front and center on her website:

> What many people don't realize is that your Attachment Style is one of the most influential forces in a relationship. This means that the success—or failure—of a relationship is largely determined by your

> Attachment Style ... [it] also impacts your friendships, familial relationships, and workplace dynamics ... Each Style has their own beliefs, perceptions, ways that they process emotions.[3]

Fifty percent of the population has a secure attachment style, which is developed by the age of two. These people most likely grew up with securely attached parents who CONSISTENTLY showed up for their needs, taught them healthy boundaries and emotion regulation, and demonstrated stability. The other 50 percent of us have one of three insecure attachment styles (which we can change, by the way).

This doesn't mean the 50 percent of us with insecure attachment styles were raised in abusive environments with parents who didn't love them. Some were, but not all. We don't know what we don't know. Even the well-intentioned parent who chooses to co-sleep with their child risks creating an insecure attachment. Parents who are absent a lot due to work or who are emotionally unavailable, leaving the children to fend for themselves, risk the same.

Our attachment style doesn't necessarily equate to an upbringing that was *toxic* or *abusive*. It can be more a matter of ignorance. It's rarely the intention of parents to harm their children. They are simply doing what they were taught to do.

And so here is more proof that children are not resilient. Children learn to cope with their circumstances in whatever way they can to avoid pain and gain pleasure. I've been stigmatized, and I have also ignorantly stigmatized others. I was stigmatized by my family when they avoided my emotional struggles and sexual trauma. It wasn't their intention to hurt me; they weren't trying to inflict more pain. They were doing what they thought was the right thing: to "let it go." My ex-husband stigmatized my mental health by blaming it for our marital issues. I stigmatized myself with that same negative belief and truly believed I was broken. I didn't talk to anyone about my mental health because I was ashamed and embarrassed. We didn't know any better because we weren't aware.

I now fully understand and accept that my mental instability back then was not the only reason for my failed marriage. There were many

---

3. https://attachment.personaldevelopmentschool.com/?utm_source=sitenavigation

factors. My attachment style stemmed from childhood, but it was not the whole picture. As Gibson says in her statement on attachment style, "The success—or failure—of a relationship is largely determined by your attachment style."

I am not responsible for my upbringing. None of that was my fault. But I am responsible for my adult life. I have spent years working on myself to become more secure. It hasn't been easy, and I still have my moments. But simply knowing I have the ability to change has empowered me.

It's Okay to Not Be Okay Sometimes

Many people who have never battled depression believe that talking of suicide is just a bid for attention. "If someone really wants to do it, they just do it," they say. Unfortunately, that is true SOMETIMES. Many "unskilled" people, by which I mean *people who have not learned effective habits and tricks to get what they want and need*, may play the suicide card for reasons of manipulation. Other times, it's a cry for help, a way for a person to be heard. It's when they stop talking about it that we should be worried.

- Suicide was the tenth leading cause of death in the U.S in 2020.[4]
- 46 percent of people who died by suicide in 2020 had a diagnosed mental health condition.[5]

I am a self-development addict. I love psychology, and I love learning about human behavior. I believe in the power of therapy. I have experienced many types of therapy, including psychotherapy, better known as "talk therapy." (Here we go again, using the word "psycho" in our treatment naming. Insert eye roll here.)

Other therapies I have experienced are Rapid Resolution Therapy (RRT), DBT, and neurofeedback therapy—all of which I go into in

---

4. NIMH » Suicide (nih.gov)
5. https://www.cdc.gov/vitalsigns/suicide/

more detail in a later chapter. But some of my best "therapy" came from self-help books and personal development seminars, which I also discuss.

I believe in Western medicine, and I believe medication should be used when absolutely necessary. Sadly, it's become the go-to solution for patients and doctors. These antidepressants or "antipsychotic" medicines can become crutches, labels, and excuses for us to stay stuck. Stuck with our perceived brokenness. Stuck with these stigmas. Stuck masking our pain and ignoring our mental health.

Going back to the beginning of this chapter, let's try it from a different perspective. Let's take an example to an extreme for the sake of getting a more clearly delineated view. For a moment, pretend that every person with a mental disorder is likely to bite off your face and enjoy it with a glass of chianti. Of course, we should avoid dangerous individuals, and that's where the stigma offers protection. *But what if we also were to provide a little bit of compassion and understanding toward them?* It does not require you to agree with cannibalism to simply understand that something happened that made them that way. Something traumatic and horrific. And usually, the more serious the mental illness, the more serious the trauma that caused it.

Resources

If you are curious about your attachment style, there are many websites that offer quizzes and results. Psychologytoday.com and personaldevelopmentschool.com are two insightful resources to get you started.

4

Spread Your Wings and Follow Your Dreams

You'll see it when you believe it.

Dr. Wayne Dyer

There was a time when I believed I was "nothing more than just a wife and stay-at-home mom." Although I believed those were the only roles or occupations possible for me, it doesn't mean that I didn't value them. Fulfilling these roles is among the toughest, most meaningful jobs there are, in my view. The problem for me was that I came to believe these were the *only* jobs I was capable of fulfilling.

I believed I couldn't make it in the world in any way that would require me to take care of myself independently because I wasn't smart enough, driven enough, educated enough, or experienced enough. I just wasn't enough. Despite having been acknowledged and promoted quickly at nearly every company I worked for prior to becoming a mom, I believed I wasn't capable of anything else but being a mom and a wife. So that's what I focused on and that's what I became. Or so I tried ...

My Old Belief System ... aka My BS

There was a time when I was called a "Stepford wife." And believe it or not, there was a time when I thought that was the best compliment you could give me. One of my favorite TV shows was *Desperate Housewives*, and Bree Van de Kamp was my favorite housewife—the one I compared myself to. Sure, she's a little uptight, and extremely conservative, a little obsessive ... But she was member of the National Rifle Association, she cooked lavish meals à la Martha Stewart, she grew the most beautiful hydrangeas, and she really knew how to make a bed look like it was straight out of *Better Homes and Gardens* magazine. Bree was a perfectionist. She was my version of a perfect wife and mother.

I used to make desserts and take them to my husband's office early in his career when I was a mom to "just" one child. I was the event planner for his company, and I put together some fantastic holiday parties and company barbecues. I took great pride in my successful events. I volunteered as a room mother every single year at my children's school and was lead room mom more than once. I chaperoned more field trips than I can even count, including ones where I found myself standing in ocean water at the Mote Marine Laboratory & Aquarium with critters swimming all around me. Anyone who knows me knows that I do not like being in natural waters because of such critters ... but I did it. I was on the PTA and chaired multiple committees over the years.

I created home crafts with my children and helped them make some awesome gifts for holidays. I planned and executed some spectacular birthday parties for my family which included real horses, custom cakes, DJs, and other live entertainment, and hand-selected menus, often cooked and put together by me. Halloween is my favorite holiday, and I was known for putting on quite the party every October, with trophies and prizes for the costume contest that so many took very seriously.

I made baby food in bulk ... from scratch. I learned to cook gourmet dinners as I watched Giada De Laurentiis, Emeril Lagasse, and Rachel Ray. I chopped up fresh herbs and spices for hours-long meal preparations. I took pride in our homes (a couple were in the 4000- to 5000-square foot range), and I kept them clean, top to bottom, all by myself. Eventually, I started full-time homeschooling, which I knocked out of the ballpark as well! I planned some really fun family vacations, including a 3500-mile, three-week road trip that included my personally creating and binding homeschool materials for each state we drove through.

Like me, Bree lost herself. Her perfectionism imploded on her. Don't get me wrong, I love the idea of any person wanting to be the best spouse and parent they can be. But as with anything, there has to be a balance, and we mustn't neglect ourselves in the process.

Although it was my intention to be the best wife and mother I could be, it was not my intention to lose myself along the way ... and that's exactly what happened. As the years went on, my circle became so small that all I had were my husband and children, and I put them on pedestals. I focused more on our home and children and less on myself and my marriage, while my husband focused more on work ... among other things.

We were both on autopilot, just going through the motions of life. We didn't mean to neglect or betray each other, but we did. I am not taking all the responsibility; we both made some poor and hurtful choices that led to our divorce. There was a time when my husband's business travels were viewed by me as a day off from making my usual standard of dinner. Instead, I was set free to tinker in my craft room or watch HGTV all night. That evolved into my obsessively wondering why his phone was being turned off during these travels.

We had grown so far apart, and the lack of appreciation on both sides was cancerous. Eventually, I was nothing but a lonely, depressed housewife and stay-at-home mom with no self-esteem, living with a man I no longer loved. One moment, I was running four miles a day, and years later, I was fifty pounds overweight and avoiding the world. I was allowing myself to be treated unfairly by people, as I lacked healthy boundaries. Heck, I don't think I had any boundaries at all. I tolerated things I never should have permitted. Gradually, I became somebody I didn't recognize. Somebody I didn't like.

Our Shadow Side

Everyone you meet is fighting a battle you know nothing about. Be kind.

Robin Williams

Fact: We all struggle with something in our lives. As one problem or situation is resolved, it seems another one is right behind it, and sometimes it's all stacked against us at once. We all have insecurities—every single person. If you say you don't, you are lying to yourself. I don't care how pretty you are, how smart you are, how much money or success you have ... we all have problems, and we all have insecurities. You can be confident and strong in one area and fully insecure in another area of life. And that's okay. We can't learn everything, but we can learn anything and do the best we can.

Another fact: We all have a choice on how we deal with our insecurities. Most of us believe that beautiful people with big egos about their looks are very confident. In reality, the overconfident ego is, more often than not, overcompensating for another insecurity that doesn't pertain to their looks ... or maybe it does. Either way, it's still an insecurity, and we all have them. There is a difference between healthy insecurities (nobody is perfect) and those insecurities that become toxic to ourselves and others.

I love psychology. I have loved it ever since I was a junior in high school after taking Psychology 101. Carl Jung is my favorite psychologist to read about. We all have what Jung refers to as our *shadow side*. Before I learned that, I would call it our *dark side* or our demons. I noticed early on that I had a side I didn't like as well as sides I didn't like about others. It's the negative programming in our subconscious mind that was learned to avoid pain and gain pleasure ... or deal with our problems, insecurities, or uncomfortable situations. Our shadow side is not pretty, but we all have one, AND we all have the power to learn to control it. Once we acknowledge it, of course.

Here's how Jung himself describes our shadow:

> The change of character brought about by the uprush of collective forces is amazing. A gentle and reasonable being can be transformed into a maniac or a savage beast. One is always inclined to lay the blame on external circumstances, but nothing could explode in us if it had not been there. As a matter of fact, we are constantly living on the edge of a volcano ...
>
> Unfortunately there can be no doubt that man is, on the whole, less good than he imagines himself or wants to be. Everyone carries a shadow, and the less it is embodied in the individual's conscious life, the blacker and denser it is. If an inferiority is conscious, one always has a chance to correct it. Furthermore, it is constantly in contact with other interests, so that it is continually subjected to modifications. But if it is repressed and isolated from consciousness, it never gets corrected.[1]

That's pretty deep and pretty accurate, in my opinion.

We all develop and learn negative patterns or habits that we use to deal (or not deal) with our emotions, thoughts, and situations. Some stonewall or avoid their problems altogether, keeping their minds and lives busy. Some use substance abuse or self-medicate in other ways. Some hide behind a busy schedule because for some reason, in today's society, busy is "Godly."

Depression and anxiety also cause a stream of unhealthy behaviors, including lack of motivation and low self-worth. When we think of ourselves as lowly, our tolerance level is raised, and we allow others to mistreat us. We continue the abuse with our negative internal dialogue about ourselves and about others.

Our attachment styles are activated, leading to injurious skills and patterns that cause more self-harm than we realize. Some of us become people pleasers, never saying no or speaking our truth just to avoid conflict, all while adding more stress onto ourselves and becoming resentful. Addictions can often go unnoticed because of the high level of tolerance we develop or how deeply we let the habit become

---

1. Carl Jung, "Psychology and Religion" (1938). In CW 11: *Psychology and Religion: West and East.*

ingrained. We are addicted to our phones, our jobs, our TV series, food, and even positive things like working out or self-development.

Our emotions and mindsets can become addictive as well. Some develop addictions to anger, anxiety, negativity, or even sadness. We can become addicted to gossiping or arguing. It becomes our base and go-to behavior. Research Professor Brené Brown refers to gossip as a "hot-wire to connection." The negative inner dialogue eventually spills over into every part of our lives. Some people are addicted to suffering and don't even realize it because it's all they know. The characteristics are never-ending.

We've all been in denial from time to time. Is it possible you are in denial about who you really are? Are you honest about your shadow side? Are you in denial about your full potential?

Like attracts like: Our dark side has low emotional intelligence and can become very powerful. The more we ignore it and the more we feed it, the more powerful and heavy it becomes. And with that comes more negativity because like attracts like. The more miserable we are, the more miserable we act and the more misery we attract.

We have so many "whys" (excuses) for our shadow sides. Our upbringing ... our neglectful parent ... the bullies at school ... our lying, cheating partner ... our backstabbing best friend who slept with our lying, cheating partner ... the list goes on to explain why we developed these behaviors. How often do we ask ourselves, *Why do they do what they do? Why do I do what I do?*

By no means am I saying that, when boundaries are crossed, we shouldn't step up for ourselves. And there are times when some space is needed between individuals, without letting it deteriorate into a psychologically abusive maneuver such as with stonewalling. But without balance and healthy skills, our shadow side can take over and become addictive, just like anything else in life.

We cannot change what we do not acknowledge.

Dr. Phil

I knew I wasn't in a good place. After separating from my husband, I soon lost all the family I had living nearby, and I felt so alone. My mother died less than a year after I left my husband. There I was at another all-time low in my life and wondering what the hell I could do to overcome this obstacle. I was so tired of therapy by this time. I was energetically and mentally exhausted by reliving and healing old wounds from childhood and my marriage. I just wanted to be me again. But did I ever really know who that was? I just wanted to be happy.

And that's when I found Alma, a life and health coach whose picture online looked so welcoming and gentle that, after a consultation, I hired her. It was August, and we were meeting in person ... outside, at a park in sweaty-ass Central Florida. The sky was blue and the air was thick. And I painfully remember the girl I was that day.

My mom had passed away the month prior. I was going through an ugly divorce and failing at an attempt at a reconciliation. I was trying desperately to hold on to a marriage and keep my family whole for a million wrong reasons, all of which I was unaware of. My emotions were nearly impossible to control because I was bipolar ... or so I believed.

I don't remember exactly what I was wearing on that hot day, but I am positive it was very comfortable and stretchy. I was so uncomfortable in my skin that I hid behind my weight and behind my oversized clothes, hoping that nobody would pay any attention to me. Hair buns became my signature, not only because it was easier, but because my hair was thinning tremendously from stress and too many medications, including preventative migraine therapy. Makeup was probably a no-go, and not because I felt confident without it but because I just didn't give a shit.

My thoughts were constantly negative and self-judgmental. I was receiving advice from everyone around me on what I should and shouldn't do. All I'd heard from my partner was how I needed to *do better*. Retail therapy and other outside sources had been an obsession. I was miserable.

I had tried my best to mask my inner misery over the years, but I couldn't any longer. I wasn't sleeping well because I had to go to the bathroom three to four times a night due to the overwhelming amount of water I was drinking each day thanks to the 1,200 mg of lithium I was taking. Lithium is a salt, and salt makes us thirsty.

I felt alone and desperate for answers, and to find them, I needed something different. Therapy was great, and I healed a lot through that process. BUT I WAS DONE! I am forever grateful and I believe in therapy 100 percent ... but I was still lost, wondering, *Who the fuck am I?* Who was I besides an ex-wife and a mother? Where was this person I was looking for? Why could I not control my anxiety no matter how medicated I was? I had to find out. I had to do *something different.*

I walked over to the tree where Alma waited, laid my portfolio down on the weathered picnic table, and got started loving myself again.

Within a couple of weeks of coaching with Alma, I was already starting to feel better. And all I had to do was be gentle with myself, take baby steps ... starting with my mindset. I went from a fixed or narrow mindset to an open mindset. One year later, as I continued to work with my amazing coach, I finally found the courage to let go of my belief system—wherein I'd been convinced I was disordered. I weaned myself off all medications with the assistance of a medical doctor.

Today, I am not only an imperfectly amazing mom, but I am also an outstanding life and health coach, author, and blogger. I accept myself as I am. I understand that not everyone on this planet will like me, and I am okay with that. I am also okay with letting people go who do not lift me up and support me the way I support them. I am okay with not having family nearby because I have become a badass, strong, independent woman, and I got this. I feel mentally and emotionally stronger than I have ever been, and I have never been more proud of myself. I know my mom and dad are proud of me too.

Step into Yourself

Yes, I believed I was good ONLY at being a wife and mother. And because I believed that, I behaved it. When people would ask me what I did, even though I was great at fulfilling these roles, I would respond with "I'm *just* a stay-at-home mom." I devalued my own job, the one in which I took so much pride.

Alma started bringing some of my limiting beliefs to the surface with simple questions.

She would ask, "What does holding on to the bipolar label do for you?" or "Why do you think you are hiding behind your weight?"

"I'm not!" I insisted.

I didn't realize how many lies I was believing about myself.

If you would have told me five years ago that I would have my own business and publish a book, I may have been inspired because they've both been on my goal list for years, but I definitely would've been skeptical. If I had been told that I would be a life and health coach, helping empower women and have an entire business map of multiple businesses, surrounded by a group of amazing and supportive peers, or that I would be living the life of an independent, high-value woman while maintaining multiple households, happily and successfully co-parenting with my ex-husband ... I would have thought, *NO WAY can I do all that.* And here I am, killing it.

And I owe that success to myself, of course, but I could never have done it without therapy and coaching. I now have a team of coaches and other empowering women who help me stretch my potential and call me out on my BS (belief system). They help me become aware of my *blind spots* (more BS!), the things I may not be seeing while I swim around my own "fishbowl."

I have raised my standards and leveled up. That means I continue to develop and improve myself because I am a work in progress, as are we all. And it means I no longer tolerate my boundaries being crossed by anyone ... including my partner. It means I will cut people out of my life who continue to cross my boundaries and take more than they bring to the table. It doesn't mean I do not feel sad about the losses, but it means I will not be feeling guilty about it. It's forgiving myself for those I have hurt and forgiving those who hurt me. It's knowing that I will have dark moments, and even dark days, ahead of me, and also knowing those moments will not last ... not unless I allow them to.

5

Boundaries and Self-Awareness

Boundaries

Good fences make good neighbors.

Robert Frost

Boundary: *a line that marks the limits of an area; a dividing line*

What exactly is a boundary? The above definition is a good place to start. A state line is an example of a geographical boundary. Florida is on one side, Georgia is on the other. Both sides of the boundary have different names and slightly different laws that their citizens and visitors are bound to abide by; otherwise, they can face consequences.

What is a personal boundary?

According to goodtherapy.com, "Boundaries are limits people set in order to create a healthy sense of personal space. Boundaries can be physical or emotional in nature, and they help distinguish the desires, needs, and preferences of one person from another."

Personal boundaries are the rules, laws, standards, or values we set for ourselves. We have a right to set them within any relationship and within any area of our life. Unfortunately, more often than not, we have the want or need for boundaries but lack the skills to claim them and to enforce them. And typically, those of us with poorly developed personal boundaries have difficulty respecting other people's boundaries. This lack of restraint then creates in us an inclination to become resentful, angry, and bitter. These emotions can manifest in aggressive or passive-aggressive manners, even developing into other painful ailments.

Types of boundaries range from physical boundaries to sexual, emotional, financial, time, and material boundaries. There are no limits. Our personal preference for how far to go in showing public displays of affection is an example of a personal boundary. How many times a day we prefer to talk to our partner is another example. It is our responsibility to be aware of our preferences and enforce such boundaries. Being monogamous or not is a sexual boundary. Wanting to get married or have children is a personal choice, value, or boundary. And the coolest part: we can always change our minds.

One of the hardest pills I have had to swallow on my life journey so far is knowing that I do, in fact, have some control over how others treat me. If we don't like how we are treated, we have the choice to tolerate the offending behavior or eliminate it. If I tell my partner that cheating is a deal-breaker, yet I stick around after he cheats, what did I just tell him?

The way we treat ourselves is the way others will treat us too. Coworkers may bully those with limited to no boundaries because they are easy targets. Even our spouses and children can mistreat us if we allow them to. It doesn't make them bad people—it makes them human. And humans can be stupid. Humans are naturally narcissistic creatures of habit. But at the end of the day, the sometimes-painful choice of whether to respect our boundary is still up to us.

We may notice disharmony in our relationships if we try to enforce boundaries, even when we do so in a healthy way. And that's how you know you are doing something right. Most (unskilled) people don't like boundaries. People without skills at getting what they need or want may become passive, bending or breaking their own boundaries to avoid conflict or losing the connection. This behavior shows others they are free to ignore our boundaries again in the future.

Disciplining our children is another example of enforcing boundaries. Every time we give in to their tantrums (often because it's easier or we lack skills), we are showing them how far we will bend. We are all guilty of this. And if we are consistent enough, our children can hone a skill to get what they want in an unhealthy way because WE TAUGHT THEM HOW! (LOL.) Not deliberately, but we did. Quite simply, that is a way we teach others how to treat us. Enforcing boundaries is not always easy, and as with anything, it is a muscle that requires practice to strengthen.

It seems we all have individuals in our lives who deliberately cross boundaries, people who have absolutely no respect for themselves or others. I have learned through experience that it is better to lose connections to people who continually drain us, those who take far more than they give. In essence, people who do that are energy vampires siphoning off our energy.

Does it mean those particular "vampires" are all bad people? No. It just means they have learned ways to get their needs met that do not align with our needs, and that stronger boundaries must be put into place for our personal well-being. No contact is usually the best boundary for this type of toxic individual. Trust me, it's better to be alone than to have people who engage in these behaviors in our lives.

We don't have to explain why we have our boundaries, and nobody has to like them or agree with them. But people who we allow into our lives could and should respect our personal boundaries and follow them because our boundaries are not about them, just as their boundaries are not about us.

No. That is a full sentence. A person with healthy boundaries can say no to others without feeling guilty or feeling the need to explain why they are saying no. If someone pushes with questions of why and doesn't take no for an answer, that person is crossing our boundary. We then have a choice: to walk away or break our own boundaries.

Self-Awareness

Know thyself.

Aristotle or Socrates? (It's a debate ...)

***Self-awareness:** conscious knowledge of one's own character, feelings, motives, and desires*

Why do I write about self-awareness and boundaries in the same chapter? If we lack self-awareness, we lack knowledge of our preferences and skills, which we need to create and enforce boundaries.

Self-awareness goes back to our emotional intelligence. Those with a lower EQ often walk around in denial about themselves and their life, seeing things from only their own perspective (their reality). And, as with learning better EQ skills, we can choose to learn self-awareness. It's beneficial to not only understand and have pride in our strengths but also be aware of our faults and improve them.

I moved out of Illinois in my early twenties and settled in Florida. For obvious reasons of warmth, I have had many beloved guests and visitors in my homes. Of course, in "Stepford-like" fashion, I created lovely guest spaces with comfortable accommodations. I looked forward to visiting with these guests, sometimes for months ahead of time. What I couldn't understand at the time was why, a day or so after their arrival, I would become irritable and short-fused. I just thought I was a moody bitch, and that was what I told myself and others. Well, that's definitely not the case. From embarking upon my self-awareness journey, one of the things I have learned is exactly what an *introvert* is, and that I am one.

***Introvert:** a shy, reticent person (meaning reserved or quiet)*

—Oxford Languages (Google)

Introvert: *a typically reserved or quiet person who tends to be introspective and enjoys spending time alone*

—Merriam-Webster

Most people, even some in my own circle, believe this to be true. And while that's a little bit true, there's more to it.

Going by Carl Jung's and Isabel Briggs Myers's studies, what it means to be introverted is that introverts re-energize themselves in solitude. Being around other people for too long is draining—energetically and physically—for us introverts. It doesn't mean we aren't capable of being the life of the party; some introverts have that in them too. What it means is that we also need our alone time to sustain the energy to be happily around people.

Extrovert: *an outgoing, overtly expressive person*

—Oxford Languages (Google)

Extrovert: *a typically gregarious and unreserved person who enjoys and seeks out social interaction*

—Merriam-Webster

Jung's and Briggs Myers's theories postulate that extroverts re-energize themselves through other people. They like their alone time as well, but that drains them. Too much alone time for an extrovert can cause depression and other emotional distress and reduce emotion regulation.

Both introverts and extroverts, as with most things, are on a spectrum, with one-third of the population being introverted. Neither is better than the other, and both have their pros and cons that make this world go round.

With awareness of my introverted nature, I now know what to do differently with my guests. First I let them know not to take my periodic alone time as anything personal. If I have guests for a long weekend, I retreat for short bursts of alone time throughout the day and retreat again a little before bedtime to unwind. If I have guests for a week or longer, when they venture off to do touristy stuff, I let them go without me so I can be a better hostess upon their return.

Understanding myself better also leads to my appreciating the extreme opposite side to being an introvert. I love my alone time. I am the type that can live in a small house with some pretty scenery, some food, music, and my laptop, and be completely happy ... until I'm not. There is a dark side to introversion. Mine involves becoming too much of a hermit and resorting to unhealthy habits of social anxiety and depression. After three or four days, if I notice I haven't left my house (I work from home), I make a point of going for a drive and getting coffee, just for a change of scene and human contact.

For me, working remotely and meeting with my clients, coaches, and friends via FaceTime or Zoom is a dream. But there has to be balance, and that's probably why I am drawn to extroverts. Those outgoing people keep me amongst human civilization and bring out my life-of-the-party side.

What's Your Type?

It is up to each person to recognize his or her true preferences.

Isabel Briggs Myers

MBTI: In the early weeks of working with my clients, I have them take the Myers-Briggs Type Indicator personality test, aka MBTI.[1] When I first took this test myself years ago, I wasn't surprised by what I read about myself, but I felt a sense of relief knowing I wasn't alone.

First let's talk a little bit about the MBTI because it is a fun topic. This personality test was developed in the 1940s by Isabel Briggs Myers and her mother, Katharine Briggs, based on the theories of none other than my favorite, Carl Jung.

1. https://www.myersbriggs.org/my-mbti-personality-type/mbti-basics/

It is broken down into sixteen personality types in combinations from four categories:

1. (I) Introverted or (E) Extroverted: Your preference of how to spend your energy and attention
2. (S) Sensing or (N) Intuition: Your preference on processing information
3. (T) Thinking or (F) Feeling: Your preference on making decisions
4. (J) Judging or (P) Perceiving: Your preference on structure

To use myself as an example, I am classified as an INFJ. And it's no wonder I felt weird my entire life. INFJ is one of the rarest of the sixteen personalities, comprising 1–3 percent of the world's population, and less than half of those people are women. We are a fascinating bunch in our own ways. We have our unique strengths, and of course, our unique shadow sides.

Growing up, I considered myself unusual, even strange. I would be reclusive because I had such a difficult time relating to others. (I love and embrace my oddities nowadays.) My sense of intuition is pretty uncanny, very psychic-like at times.

My learning about my INFJ personality (nickname "the Counselor") amped up my healing and development journey. Not only did I start to understand myself better, but others too. I am by no means an expert in the MBTI (yet) as that is a science in itself, and one must go through a process of certification. Nonetheless, it has been a useful tool in my personal life. The guidance one can gain from this tool is absolutely fascinating to me.

The Enneagram: The Enneagram is another personality test, one that I am less familiar with, but I find it very interesting. I like the way it explains our personalities when we are at our best and when we are at our worst, and the way we overlap with other personality types. Our personalities are always on a spectrum, and we can only work at always doing the best we can each day. There is a lot of reading material available on this subject if you are interested in exploring it further.

DiSC: The DiSC assessment is a popular personal assessment tool used across many industries to help determine communication style, strength, and weaknesses. DiSC is an acronym for the personality profiles considered in the model: dominance, influence, steadiness, and conscientiousness.[2]

Heck, even our astrological natal birth chart can bring enhanced levels of self-awareness. There's more than may seem obvious to be explored with the question "What's your sign?" as we all have several signs in our birth chart, which, in relation to each other, explain much of what makes us unique. My own natal chart says that I am independent and autonomous, I love self-development, I am unique and unusual, and writing is in the stars for me. Coincidence?

Taking the Wheel of Our Lives

We are in charge of our own lives and our own happiness. Mastering new skills that regulate our emotions helps us raise our EQ. The higher our emotional intelligence, the greater chance we have to acknowledge our shadow side and start changing it. We also raise awareness about our boundaries and learn the skills to enforce them. It's not easy. Our subconscious mind dislikes change and will seek to sabotage our best efforts. It takes consistency, patience, and time.

Think back to childhood, or even as an adult, and recall how you have treated people differently from one another in terms of the respect each commanded. As a child, I would smart off to my grandma sometimes when I was feeling feisty. I knew how far I could go with her before I would get in trouble. But my grandfather? Never happened. I wouldn't even smart off to my grandma if he were anywhere around because I would instantly be put into check. Just my name said in a certain tone with a certain look, and I knew what was up.

I remember a time when I was fourteen years old and I was living with my grandparents. Our answering machine received an automated message that I was not in school that day. While eating dinner, my

2. https://www.discprofile.com/what-is-disc
https://justastrologythings.com/pages/chart/
https://astro.cafeastrology.com/natal.php

grandfather confronted me, and I assured him I was in every class. He was calm, and he didn't believe me. As I started crying because he was grounding me, I tried to interrupt him to tell him again I had been in school. The second he raised his voice and he warned me to not talk back, I stopped talking. I knew better because he would follow through with consequences, which kept me from crossing his boundary even when I knew I was right. The next morning, my grandma and I walked into the administration office, and they confirmed it was a computer error. I was, in fact, provably in school. (Little did we know I was going to master truancy later.)

As we consistently learn and strengthen new skills that work for us, and our EQ level is raised, everything begins to shift—a little at a time. Even as I am writing this chapter, I just did the happy dance after learning my son is bringing his siblings home today after school, meaning I don't have to leave my house ALL day if I don't want to. I love that little treat because then I can continue writing in my happy place.

We teach others how we will tolerate being treated. We may want to be treated differently, but unless we are aware of and uphold our personal boundaries, we will be treated in ways we do not prefer or enjoy. And the way we allow others to treat us is a reflection of how we internally treat ourselves. Sometimes, we realize our own toxic behaviors are partly to blame, and we can learn to work through them and establish healthier behaviors. We all have some toxic or unhealthy behaviors we've learned to get our needs met.

It is up to us to learn and understand why we do the things we do, then use the self-knowledge to reprogram our brain and raise our EQ. Self-awareness creates better understanding of the boundaries we want in place, and focusing on that is just one of the many little steps on our path to intrinsic happiness.

Resources

I love online tests and quizzes that help me learn more about myself. The emotional intelligence test is offered from several websites on the internet, some free, some not. The MBTI test can be taken at www.mbtionline.com and costs around $50. I include it in my coaching packages, and my clients have really enjoyed learning about themselves. IQ tests are available as well as depression and anxiety tests. You name it. And be sure to check out my website at www.jenslifecoaching.com.

Remember, we can't appreciate or change or develop what we do not acknowledge.

6

The Power of Forgiveness

What would you think if I were to tell you I have a superpower? Would you laugh if that superpower happens to be forgiveness? It might seem like a boring gift to many, if not most. And it will definitely feel useless to anyone who hasn't experienced its magic. As you move toward forgiving someone, it may feel like you are just going through the motions. Until one day ... you feel free.

What is forgiveness exactly?

Forgiveness comes from the need to let go of negative and hurtful emotions we feel toward another person or entity for some wrongdoing. Some of those emotions are anger, heartbreak, rejection, resentment, disgust, sadness, abandonment, or even remorse.

While these emotions are negative, they do serve a purpose. Our emotions, if used properly, are part of the grief and healing process or among our natural instincts as tools for survival. It's okay to feel any emotion that arises within us. It's okay to hold on to those emotions sometimes as we go through the motions ... toward forgiveness. Yet if we do not learn to control our emotions and understand them, they can become addictive. Over time, these useful emotions have the potential to become toxic.

Anger is a very powerful and necessary emotion. We all feel it. To the surprise of many, it is in fact a *secondary emotion*. I know what some of you who are hearing this for the first time are thinking, *No way! That bitch in the BMW pissed me off the other day when she almost sideswiped me on the highway!*

And rightfully so! Anger is the predominantly felt emotion, and still, the secondary. In this situation, anger is immediately felt *after* feeling the primary emotion of fear—fear of getting into a car accident and potentially causing harm to ourselves and others.

Anger has a purpose. Anger releases a cocktail of chemicals that helps us in many situations when we may need our fight or flight skills, including this specific situation of "the bitch in the BMW." Depending on how well developed our anger-management skills are, we can hold on to that anger and carry it into the rest of our day like a ripple effect, or we can keep calm and not ruin our day by taking the incident personally. Besides, we have no frigging clue why the person behind the wheel was driving recklessly in the first place ... maybe she was rushing to the hospital to say goodbye to her dying father. We automatically assume we know it's because she was running late or it's by default because she drives a BMW.

Same thing goes for bigger issues like heartbreak, trauma, or the loss of a loved one. Anger still serves a purpose, and it is still a secondary emotion to a list of primary emotions such as sadness, abandonment, rejection ... the list goes on. It's just part of the process of *emotion regulation*. In the mental health world it's referred to as "riding the wave." They come and they go.

> *Holding on to anger is like drinking poison and expecting the other person to die.*
>
> Often attributed to Buddha

So what does it mean to truly forgive someone? It starts with acknowledging the pain and finally accepting the situation for what it is. It is understanding that no amount of anger is ever going to erase what happened. And no number of apologies will ever make it go away. As adults, we all have some responsibility for our pain, even if it's just 10 percent. Forgiveness begins with our reflecting on the situation and the persons involved and taking accountability for our part.

Being willing to forgive means having the courage to show compassion to those who hurt us and understanding that they, too, are struggling with something, and that is why they hurt us. It's acknowledging and accepting that we are all human, and we all make mistakes. It's realizing that the way others act is a reflection of themselves in their current state of mind, and it has nothing to do with us. It's acknowledging that we all have a shadow side. It's reclaiming our power and finding inner peace. It's freedom. And it's one of my superpowers.

What Forgiveness Is NOT

Forgiving someone who hurt us doesn't excuse their actions. The men who sexually abused me when I was growing up were 100 percent wrong. Just as their horrible actions are a reflection of them, forgiving them is a reflection of me. It benefits me *first and foremost*. It benefits all of us first and foremost when we forgive others. But forgiveness most definitely does not justify the hurtful action.

One of the mantras of DBT is this: *We are all doing our best, and we can do better*. When my therapist first said that to me in regard to how my mother behaved while I was growing up, I was like "DAMN STRAIGHT, she could've done better! And no, she was not doing the best she could!!"

I was so angry and resentful toward my mom. I blamed her for doing a poor job raising me, for ushering me into all of those traumatic experiences. I even directed blame at her for the failure of my marriage because I believed that, had she been a better mother and taught me better skills, I would've had better skills to keep my marriage together. I blamed her for having poor judgment and bringing me around the men who hurt me as a child.

When I started intense therapy, she was dying from COPD and emphysema resulting from years of self-inflicted abuse. I was so resentful because, along with her having created my troubled past, I now had to watch her slowly die and be taken away from me too soon because "she was doing the best she could."

Fuck that, I thought. I would never treat my children the way she did. How dare she be so selfish?

Fast-forward to today. As I reflect on my parenthood adventure thus far, I have not inflicted anywhere near that extent of trauma toward my children, but I am still responsible for some trauma in their lives. Their parents are divorced, and they've witnessed us fight too many times in the past. I have yelled at them—for some good reasons, and at times without good reasons. (Kids don't understand the difference until they become parents.) Sometimes I am short with them, and every once in a while, I really lose it. I have not been a perfect mom. No one is a perfect mom or dad, and those imperfections can cause pain in our children.

One time when I was in fifth grade, I went to my mom on a Sunday evening right before bedtime with the dreaded "forgotten project." The assignment was to learn how to follow a recipe and bring in the finished product. When I told this to my mom, she was not happy. She was quite frustrated, in fact, and I remember feeling bad for causing that. Nonetheless, she and I together made a coffee cake from scratch, and I took it to class the following day. I never forgot something like that again.

Thirty years later, my oldest son, who's a teen, pulls this crap on me time and time again. Each time, I get frustrated with him. And of course I stop what I am doing and I help him. My frustration shows differently each time, depending on the day.

Did you know that the human race is the only species that punishes for the same misdeed over and over? We punish loved ones and ourselves repeatedly for the same mistakes. We judge, we blame, we rationalize, and we project our own pain out into the world. Who are we really hurting?

(Unskilled) Hurt People Hurt People

We judge ourselves by our intentions and others by their behavior.

Stephen R. Covey

I believe most people have good intentions. My parents didn't intend to hurt me with their lack of parenting skills. Given that they barely had their own life skills operational, how could they have known how to properly raise children with emotional intelligence and relationship skills? Or been aware enough to understand that every single behavior, good or bad, can have a great impact on their children? How was my mom to know how to be an effective parent when she herself was raised by a mother who was married at nineteen and had her first child ten months later?

What the DBT mantra really means is this: *Yes, we are all doing the best we can (with the skills we have), and we can do bette*r. And *our best* changes—day to day, situation to situation.

My mother did the best she could with the tools she had. She raised two kids by herself without any kind of support from my dad. She did everything she could to keep us fed and sheltered, even if that meant leaving us to live with other family members for months at a time. As for my dad, his leaving hurt all of us. His absence over the years brought a lot of pain, but then again, so did his presence. He had his own shadow side he was battling. He was a drunk. He was unemployed more often than not. He was miserable, and his wife and kids wanted nothing to do with him. I guess you could say we emotionally abandoned him too.

My dad's lack of presence in our lives wasn't because of anything we did. He didn't fail to show up in our lives because he wanted to fail us. He didn't show up because, with the limited skills he had developed, he couldn't. He was projecting out to the world what he felt inside. Did his behaviors hurt? Absolutely. Did they have a great impact on my life, both negative and positive? Yes. I was able to forgive him knowing that he was doing the best he could with the resources he had. That became especially clear when he was on his deathbed and asked me on Messenger why we had lost touch over the years. His perception was his reality.

The last time I saw my dad was when I was twenty-two years old—on my wedding day. The time before that had been when I was in high school. He found enough strength and courage to come to his daughter's wedding, where he was acknowledged only as a guest and not as the father of the bride. He found the courage to face a room full of people who had wrongfully judged him, as well as face the new judgments that arose from the guests who, until then, weren't familiar with our story.

But he did it. And he smiled. We took pictures, he danced with me, and he told me he loved me. I never saw him again. He never met any of his grandchildren. He passed away in hospice when I was thirty-nine years old.

One of my favorite memories of my dad was when I was in first or second grade. My parents were still together, and it was Halloween time. I wanted to be Strawberry Shortcake but we couldn't find that costume, so I settled for going as Smurfette. A few days before the holiday, my dad came home with a Strawberry Shortcake costume. I was so happy and felt loved by him.

What is an apology? Do we really need it? We do not need an apology to forgive. In fact, apologies directed our way aren't for us; they alleviate the other person's guilt and remorse. My mom apologized to me nearly a decade before I decided to forgive her. My sexual abusers will never have the chance to apologize, and I am okay with that. All we need is some time and self-awareness and the healing superpower of forgiveness.

Setting Your Intention to Forgive

We start with asking ourselves some serious questions. Why should we forgive? Why do we want to forgive? Set the intention and ride the wave. It doesn't happen overnight. But with the right skills, we can let go of the pain that is haunting us.

Trust me, forgiving is not an easy task. Martin Luther King, Jr., said, "We must develop and maintain the capacity to forgive. He who is devoid of the power to forgive is devoid of the power to love." Read that again.

And whether or not you are Christian, the Bible speaks of forgiveness consistently. Jesus washed Judas's feet, for crying out loud.

> *But if you don't forgive others, then your Father in heaven will not forgive the wrongs you do.*
>
> Matthew 6:15

The last person I ever wanted to forgive was my ex-husband. *No way! He was a jerk, and he did me dirty in our marriage and even worse in our divorce! Why would I ever forgive him*? So I thought. And yet, he's where the shift happened for me.

A couple of years ago, I attended a Tony Robbins event in Florida. Tony has become my virtual dad and one of my favorite mentors. I just hear his voice and I am already inspired to be a better version of me. Anyway, he talks all about this forgiveness stuff and asks some bold questions. Questions like "If you continue with this pattern or behavior for the rest of your life, how will you be in one, five, ten, or twenty years from now? How are the relationships around you affected by this anger?"

Robbins created a unique and powerful mental exercise to examine the impact of our limiting beliefs called the Dickens process (referring to Charles Dickens's character Ebenezer Scrooge), which led me down the mental path of visual hell. A path I was choosing, no matter how justified the choice (as I believed it was).

One of my Dickens processes was imagining how my kids would react to me over the years should I continue to be angry at their father. I saw my kids hating me and resenting me ... the same way I had felt about my own parents.

Through my tears and potential pain as I imagined it, I realized that I needed to forgive my ex. Why? Let me list the ways: Because my kids deserve it. Because I deserve it. It's good for my soul and good for my inner peace. It's healthier for my future romantic relationships. It's beneficial for my own relationships with my children. It will ease their healing from the trauma of the divorce I am partly responsible for, permitting them to feel emotionally safe with both parents in spite of that trauma. None of which I had growing up. Did my ex deserve my forgiveness? No, not really, and he probably didn't even care. But I deserved it. My children deserved it.

That day, I set the intention to forgive him. I prayed and meditated and journaled. I read books, particularly one of my go-tos, *The Four Agreements* by Don Miguel Ruiz. I was finally able, at an energetic level, to show my ex some compassion and understanding and to accept that his behaviors are a reflection of himself just like my behaviors are a reflection of myself.

First, Self-Forgiveness

During this journey, I also forgave myself. We don't usually think to forgive ourselves. Yet we can be our own worst critic, beating ourselves up mentally with constant self-judgment and negative self-talk.

I remember the guilt and remorse I felt because of having inflicted some of my pain onto my ex-husband, including through having had an affair of my own. I was deeply angry with myself for causing so much pain to so many people around me. After accepting that he, too, had reasons to need to forgive me, I was able to forgive him, down to my soul. But whether he chooses to forgive me is part of his own personal journey.

I was now choosing to come from a place of peace and to project that outward. While this personal choice doesn't make any of the hurtful actions either party did okay, quite simply, it does show grace to the other person, regardless of the behaviors. When I forgave myself, I forgave him. When I forgave him, I started to behave differently toward him. The ripple effect continues to flow onto my children with the gift of a healthy co-parenting relationship and emotional stability.

The blame-shame-guilt cycle is vicious. The self-abuse humans inflict is traumatizing. I was preparing to say goodbye to my mom while she was withering away in front of me during the last years of her life. There was even a time when part of me wanted her to die because I felt she had become such a burden to me.

I lied to my mother's face a couple of hours before they removed her ventilator. The doctors had informed us privately that they were going to remove her breathing tube and that she was going to die because her lungs were comparable to a 180-year-old human and her body wasn't strong enough to survive. My family all agreed that we would tell her the truth, and I was to be the one to tell her. Sometimes being the strong one really sucks.

My mom was using a notepad to scribble her frustrated attempts to communicate with us, which I still have to this day. She was afraid.

"Am I going to die?" she wrote.

"Yes," I said.

"What if I don't remove the tube?"

"You will never breathe on your own again." I explained to her that living that way was not a healthy option.

"I don't want to die." This time, tears were in her eyes.

"I know, Mom. We don't want you to die either."

I was sensing that she was considering not removing the tube for as long as she could manage. And as much as I didn't want my mother to die, I couldn't let her live that way.

"Do I have any chance at all to breathe on my own?" She looked at me with hopeful eyes.

"Yes, you have a small chance," I lied. I will never forget her immediate response. She dropped her pen and paper, held up her hands, and agreed to remove the tube.

Her last words to me were, "Hi, baby," uttered in a whisper after they had removed her ventilator and were transporting her to hospice. Her eyes were sunken in, her bones protruding against her frail flesh. She closed her eyes, and they remained closed for the next five days before she took her last breath.

I tried to say goodbye to her. I tried letting her go. I remember sleeping in the recliner at her bedside during that week, wanting more time with her. After several days in hospice, one night I went home to sleep and left my grandmother alone with her dying daughter. I knew she was going to die that night. My grandmother asked me repeatedly to stay with her, and I insisted on going home. I could not be there for my mom's last breath, I just couldn't. Instead, I selfishly left my grandmother to deal with that by herself. It is, to this day, one of my biggest regrets and an action for which I have yet to forgive myself, despite apologizing to my grandma.

And then, I had to forgive the family who left me alone to take care of my mother's estate on my own, including separating her ashes into thirds to share with my grandmother and brother. I had no idea that our cremated remains were white ash with chunky bits of bone.

Today, I would do almost anything to spend time with her. As I spent the next months after her death, cleaning out her home and sifting through her life, I forgave her a million times over. I missed her. She had kept mementos, including Christmas gifts I made her as a child or bought her from the school holiday gift shop that I was so proud of back then. She kept our school artwork, ribbons, and awards. I had no idea she still had any of these things, and when I found them, I felt so much love.

Forgiveness as a Superpower

I didn't fully forgive my mother until after her death. It happened at last while I was writing the eulogy for her celebration of life party. I just couldn't bring myself to forgive her until I first forgave myself for being so angry and projecting that outward while she was here. I was doing the best I could, with the tools I had ... *and I can do better.*

Why forgive the men who sexually abused me? So when I smell patchouli, the scent of one of the abusers, I am no longer thrown into a spiral of traumatizing memories that linger for hours or days. So I can finally be truly intimate with my partner, giving him all of me, and have a loving, trusting sexual relationship with him that isn't haunted by my past.

Choosing to hold on to anger and resentment imprisons us and robs us of living the life we deserve. We all have hurt someone in our lives. In fact, we have all probably hurt one hundred different people, without even realizing our impact. We all deserve forgiveness.

> *You'll never know how strong your heart is until you learn to forgive those who broke it.*
>
> Anonymous

So often, I hear people say they forgive someone, but their actions don't align with those words. They continue to spread gossip and hate about the ones they claim to have forgiven. What many of us do is to suppress our feelings to the point of numbness. But that is not true forgiveness because the angry energy still sits within us.

When we spread hate about someone we "forgave," we are lying to ourselves. That behavior tells us our thoughts are not in alignment with forgiveness. It's one thing to say it and another thing to mean it.

A meditation and prayer I practice to help with forgiveness is the Hawaiian Ho'oponopono Prayer ...

~ I'm sorry. Please forgive me. Thank you. I love you. ~

It's quite challenging to start this meditation when you have sworn enemies, but with time and practice, it really does work. It's essential we accept and forgive *our trespasses* so we can then forgive others. This leads us to freedom from unnecessary suffering. Forgiveness becomes a superpower.

7

A Recipe for Happiness

The most profoundly happy days of writing this book so far have been the ones when I was staring at the computer screen, eyes filled with tears and not a single word written. You may be wondering how that can be or thinking something along the lines of *that sure doesn't sound like a happy person* ... or *some life coach you must be*. But hear me out.

I had some good momentum going with this book, and this was one of my favorite chapters—the one I was really looking forward to starting. I tacked all my notes and outlines about my own personal pursuit of happiness on the corkboard above my desk. I felt like I had a million thoughts and words floating around in my brain, and yet all I managed to punch onto the keys were a few hundred words. This went on for almost two weeks as I reorganized my desk, gazed over my sources of inspiration, pondered my outline, and even watched YouTube videos. Then suddenly, my mind turned it all into a recipe for happiness.

My planned word count for this chapter was around 3,400. After I got my momentum back, although I was still late to my deadline and my initial draft was rather disorganized given my perfectionism, I was over 4,000 words. And I could still add more.

I have chosen to be happy because it is good for my health.

Voltaire

Even when a pen is not in hand or a keyboard handy, I am almost always thinking about what I want to write. Sometimes, I am not necessarily mulling over details for this book but more for future books or potential journal and blog entries. Looking into my office is pretty much like sifting into my diary as it's filled with books and training manuals, lots of visionary inspiration, my own personal development charts that help me measure my growth, sweet Post-it Notes from my kids, a picture of me and my boyfriend. Peeking from behind my laptop screen, pinned on the cork board, is a picture of my mom and dad when they were together in semi-formal attire. And another picture of myself around the age of nine reveals a mischievous smirk on my young face. I pinned them there the day I started writing actual chapters for this book almost a year ago.

My nine-year-old self is wearing a purple plaid shirt, standing outside the brick apartment building we lived in at the time. I had already been sexually molested by the first of four men in my life to inflict that abuse on me, and I was intrinsically dealing with the ruminating thoughts that haunted me into adulthood from that horrific experience. I was doing everything in my power to forget what my subconscious hadn't already repressed. I remember wondering, as my stomach turned in disgust, if I was going to think about that trauma forever.

As I look at these pictures and daydream into the past forty-plus years of my life, my heart is full of nothing but love and gratitude. A lot of bad shit happened to me, and as an adult, I put myself through a lot more shit. But that doesn't mean I am miserable, nor does it mean I am a bad person. When I look at that picture of myself, memories flood my mind of playing outside ALL THE TIME. Running around playing tag, riding our bikes around the neighborhood, and sneaking behind one of the buildings that had a swamp so we could catch baby frogs. We lived in that apartment complex for four years, kindergarten through third grade … the longest stretch of time I ever lived in one home growing up.

Although there were some intense and scary moments, it wasn't all bad. And there were powerful and unique lessons learned. I became who I am today because of those experiences, and I love who I am. I am far from perfect but I am amazing, even on the days I may forget that, and I am always improving. And that is why I sit at the screen with tears in my eyes—because I am grateful to be alive and I am grateful for the person I am and the person I will become. Some of my experiences I do not wish on anyone. Nonetheless, I am grateful for the lessons I have learned so far.

For instance, the experience of having lived my childhood has taught me a lot of what NOT to do when it comes to parenting. I also notice the signs of "grooming," when a predator is wanting to do horrendous things to a child and their body. Because of my past trauma, I am able to protect my children slightly better than those of us who are naïve to how the sick process works and who the real monsters may be. Hint: It is not necessarily the stranger down the road listed on the sex offender app. The ones to watch out for are typically closer in our circle than we think.

Choose Your Ingredients

Happiness is a choice, and it is our own personal responsibility to find intrinsic happiness. I know many people do not agree that happiness is a choice. They think life has dealt them a bad hand and life just sucks. Or they think they always find the bad seeds in the dating pool and that rotten luck has nothing to do with what is within themselves. Not so. Life is what we make it. How happy a life we may have has nothing to do with the amount of money we make, how many friends we have, or how great our grades are. It doesn't matter how many times our spouse cheated on us or how toxic our family is or if our parent(s) were never physically around or otherwise present.

As adults, we have choices, and whether we like those choices or not, they are in fact still choices. You don't like your job? Lower your standards, change your mindset, or find a new one. You don't like yourself or your partner? Same thing. Are those always the easier choices to make? Of course not. And it's also a choice to keep on doing the same things you're doing ... and continue being unhappy.

Learning, understanding, and accepting what we can and cannot control, that is how we move forward. The simple answer to that is this: we can control *only* ourselves. But what exactly does that mean?

For starters, we control our decisions. As an American, I have a choice to vote or not vote. I have the choice to have children, to get married. As an adult, I have complete control over every behavior and action I do every single day.

Here are some of the things over which we have control:

- Our thoughts
- Our judgments
- Our emotions
- Our boundaries
- Our reactions and responses to people and situations
- The amount of time and effort we put in
- What we put into our minds
- What we put into our bodies
- Our actions and the way we treat others, including our enemies
- The way we treat our body
- Who we spend our time with
- How we spend our time
- When we sleep
- How we manage our money
- How we allow others to treat us
- Our amount of suffering
- What we say yes and no to
- Our environment and home
- Our healing from past pain and trauma
- Our emotional intelligence
- What we focus on

The list goes on and on. We have more choices and control than we realize. Yet I'm sad to say, we focus on what we cannot control. More often than not, the more out of control we are internally, the more we project that control onto others and delude ourselves.

Things we cannot control:

- What other people do
- What other people think
- What other people feel
- What other people say
- Other people's choices and lifestyles
- Other people's values and preferences
- Things from the past
- The weather

How many of us have tried to control our partners or our children, even passive-aggressively? If we are honest with ourselves, we can admit it has happened from time to time—I guarantee it. Some people are highly controlling, acting in a more aggressive manner. Either way, such behavior is a projection of our internal loss of control and insecurities. And trying to control things that are out of our control as a way of feeling in control and avoiding our own inner demons only creates emotional and relationship problems.

From my studies over the last several years and my own personal experience, I have found similarities in theories on the pursuit of happiness, and there really is a recipe for it. And as with many recipes, there are many variations to the ingredients, depending on each person, but they all start with *setting the intention to be happy.*

Bad shit is going to happen to us—it's inevitable. The more we focus on the negative, the more negativity is drawn in. The more we focus on the positive, the same dynamic is at play ... more positivity is drawn in. Depending on one's belief system, there are different names for this phenomenon. Spiritualists call this the Law of Attraction, and those who prefer a more science-based approach call it the power of the subconscious. Two amazing books to read on these topics are *The Law of Attraction: The Basics of the Teachings of Abraham* by Esther and Jerry Hicks and *The Power of Your Subconscious Mind* by Joseph Murphy,

PhD, DD. Humans really are "magical" creatures. We have a lot more intrinsic power than we realize.

Before I go into my recipe, I would like to start with a very powerful prayer that I feel validates some very important "ingredients" that I will talk about.

The Serenity Prayer (the full version)

God grant me the serenity to accept the things I cannot change,
Courage to change the things I can, and wisdom to know the difference,
Living one day at a time, enjoying one moment at a time,
Accepting hardships as the pathway to peace,
Taking, as He did, this sinful world, as it is, not as I would have it,
Trusting that He will make things right, if I surrender to His Will,
So that I may be reasonably happy in this life, and supremely happy with Him
Forever and ever in the next. Amen.[1]

I think the prayer helps explain everything in my recipe. Along with understanding and accepting what we can and cannot control, I have some additional "ingredients" or actions we can fold into our lives to create a more happy and harmonious independent life.

(Some) Ingredients for Happiness

- Setting the intention to be happy
- Learning and accepting what we can and cannot control
- Practicing gratitude daily
- Living in the present moment
- Growing in self-awareness
- Raising our EQ

---

1. Reinhold Niebuhr (1892–1971)

- Watching our thoughts
- Avoiding comparisons of ourselves to others
- Discovering and mastering our passions
- Establishing healthy personal boundaries and values
- Knowing our worth (and adding tax)
- Practicing forgiveness
- Thinking and responding nonjudgmentally
- Contributing
- Opening to spirituality and religion
- Surrounding ourselves with the right people
- Feeling our negative emotions, but not living with them
- Ceasing to care what others think about us
- Understanding and nurturing our needs, wants, and desires
- Engaging in radical acceptance
- Moving our bodies
- Being authentic
- Healing our inner child and honoring our inner rebel
- Practicing self-love, self-compassion, and self-worth
- Achieving work/life balance
- Using social media for positive
- Avoiding comparisons to others' "snapshots"

The Right Mix

I know there are more ingredients that can be added, and depending on each person's preferences and what is going in our lives, some of these things need to be nurtured more at times. But from my observations, I believe that if we do not nurture these habits and ingrain them into our lives, and do not take care of ourselves, we create inner resentment. And that, in my opinion, is one of the deadly, soul-crushing emotions we can feel that leads to anger and more unhappiness.

Limited Social Media: Losing yourself to social media is a tragic way to toxify many of the Happiness Ingredients I just shared with you. Social media can be a blessing and generate positivity and human connection, which happens to be a human need. It can even create an income. It can also create drama and draw negativity toward us. Don't get me wrong, I think social media is wonderful ... if we allow it to be. The choice is ours.

Years ago, I indulged in the dark side of social media. I enjoyed posting random things from pictures of my kids to interesting articles. I followed a lot of individuals and entities who created a lot of consistent, subtle negativity on my feeds. And that negativity eventually became a poison as I paid attention to how many likes I got and who DIDN'T like my post. I would spend a lot of time and mental energy going down the wormhole of reading strangers' comments on posts and often times getting myself caught up in some unnecessary drama and arguments that followed me around in my thoughts for days. I lost friendships because of the power I gave away.

During my divorce, I took a hiatus from the outside world, including all social media. Upon my return, I had a new life, a new mindset, and a new set of personal boundaries. What I was willing to allow into my life had changed as well. I realized that much of the energy that had been flowing into my life through social media proved itself far from beneficial for me. For instance, I do not allow politics on my feed or anything news-related or controversial. If a "friend" happens to be constantly negative and it's affecting my mood, I take them off my feed for a little while and send them positive vibes.

I no longer participate in a debate of any kind, and I definitely do not engage in any negative banter. I no longer pay any attention to my *likes* because I have learned that it doesn't matter. In fact, I get more private DMs on my coaching posts from people I have helped, and they NEVER once hit the "like" button. How many others have I helped who never said a thing? I choose to have positive posts in my feed.

Happy girls are the prettiest.

Audrey Hepburn

Positivity: Did you know that the simple act of smiling, even a fake *half-smile* (as called in dialectical behavior therapy) releases happy hormones in the brain? The brain doesn't know it is a fake smile. That's why laughing is the best medicine.

According to Vocabulary.com:

> Happiness is that feeling that comes over you when you know life is good and you can't help but smile ... Happiness is a sense of well-being, joy, or contentment. When people are successful, or safe, or lucky, they feel happiness ... different people feel happiness for different reasons. Whenever doing something causes happiness, people usually want to do more of it. No one ever complained about feeling too much happiness.

Our brain's response is more proof that the more positivity we put into our lives, the more of it we will want (referencing back to Sigmund Freud's pain and pleasure theory). It becomes the new norm for us, our new baseline. And when bad things happen (because that is inevitable), we can take the punches, go through the process, and come out on the other side ready to face the world. Life will never be perfect.

Change your habits, change your life.

Tom Corley

Integrity: Always hold true to your integrity and values, and do what makes you happy. We all have different wants, needs, and desires. If we all liked the same hobbies and music, we'd be boring as fuck. Do not judge yourself or others for their preferences. We have a choice to love who we want to love and be who we want to be. We should not have to endure the judgment or opinions of others.

Happiness doesn't just come to us. Sure, things and people can bring us joy, but true intrinsic happiness comes from within. Happiness doesn't happen after the big job promotion or after the wedding or after the baby or after that degree or after you win the lottery. Happiness is a choice. It is an intentional set of behaviors, thoughts, and habits that create internal peace and intrinsic happiness.

We will never be truly happy trying to bring it from the outside in. The only happiness that is sustainable comes from doing the hard work from the inside out. There is no other way. Yes, the new car should be celebrated. It brings great happiness ... until it doesn't. And then, something new is needed to replace the diminished joy from the draining cup of positivity we are attempting to fill externally.

Happiness comes from the little things, the big things, and the lessons in the bad things. Earlier in the book, I mentioned that I cheated during my marriage. It is not something I am proud of, and it is not something I would recommend to anyone. Nonetheless, I learned the valuable, hard lessons derived from not only the giving side of cheating, but also the receiving side. The guilt I felt for so many years was unbearable at times. After finally forgiving both myself and my ex, I now know that I will never ever cheat, nor tolerate cheating. I will do everything in my power to avoid the pain that (always) comes from cheating ... even when we aren't caught.

I have learned valuable lessons on the psychology of cheating, so even though I disagree with the act itself, I understand how and why it can happen, and I don't judge others who do it. I gathered a toolbox of new skills that helps me not fall into that slow and steady quicksand of destruction and pain ever again. Starting with my thoughts.

Today is going to be the best day because we're having hot chocolate!

Jackson (age 6)

Gratitude: The practice of gratitude is just as powerful as that of forgiveness. It's not happy people who are grateful; it is grateful people who are happy. It's one thing to say we are grateful—everyone says they are. It's completely different to actually feel grateful and behave gratefully. The more it's done, the more the gifts of gratitude start to pour over into other areas in our lives.

And what I mean by *feeling grateful* is deeply sensing the emotion behind the gratitude. If you are grateful for an accomplishment you achieved, savor it inside your soul. Nurture and love the blood, sweat, and tears that went into achieving that goal. If you are grateful for your partner, imagine your life without this wonderful person, sensing that imagined pain, and then multiply that by a hundred. Now feel the gratitude that your partner is alive in this present moment, and love that. Try feeling grateful through the eyes of a child and see how much more intensity and wonder come through. If you are grateful for having hot chocolate during your classroom Christmas party, revel in your love for that hot chocolate and share the joy.

One of our family rituals at mealtime is practicing gratitude. We each have our own journal where we write down (or draw pictures, depending on age) three things we are grateful for that day. My oldest resists this practice but he still participates. We have the option to share or not share.

It's really rewarding to look back and see all of the amazing things we have to feel grateful for. One time, when I flipped through my journal, I came across the day of my mother's sixtieth birthday. I wrote down how grateful I was to have my mother and how much I loved her.

The emotions and energies of people can be contagious. Happy people spread happiness and truly want others to be happy too. These are the people we all gravitate toward because their energy is so exuberant. Happy people fill up others' cups, rather than seeking to take from them. And that, too, fills their own cup in return. Intrinsically happy people who are grateful for all their blessings in life do not spread hate and gossip about others. They show appreciation and respect boundaries for both themselves and others.

Controlling Our Thoughts

Just as with the Buddhist quote I used earlier in this book, there is a similar verse in the Old Testament of the Bible under Proverbs 4:23–27 (ERV):

> Be careful what you think because your thoughts control your life. Don't bend the truth or say things you know are not right. Keep your eyes on the path, and look straight ahead. Make sure you are going the right way, and nothing will make you fail. Don't go to the right or to the left, and you will stay away from evil.

It's a simple skill, and yet it is not easy ... at first. Just like anything else we master, it becomes easy. Observing our thoughts, without judgment, is a mindfulness practice, and the first step to learning to control them. A thought is just a thought. No matter how "true" we perceive that thought to be, it is still just a thought. Notice the thought. You can ask yourself with curiosity where that thought is coming from and just be still.

Be mindful of the words of the wicked as they spread gossip, lies, and half-truths about others as a form of external thought control. We are not responsible for what others say, but we are responsible for what we choose to believe. We are responsible for getting *all the facts* before making decisions or judgments about others.

What would happen if we just let the thought be a thought and allowed it to float away? What if we decided not to act upon the thought or ruminate on it or add additional thoughts that create a false story? What if we reminded ourselves that we can come back to this thought at a later time?

Radical Acceptance: We have a choice to accept the things we cannot control and change or to remain stuck and be less happy than we could be. For instance, death and dying is an inevitable part of life and so are breakups and divorces. We are most likely going to lose people throughout our lives, and these situations are some of the most painful experiences on a human soul. Suppressing and denying that someone has passed on or not accepting a breakup only causes unnecessary suffering.

My mom passed away a few years ago. It was more painful than I ever imagined it would be, and I miss her more than words can describe. Sometimes, the sudden urge to call my mom comes to mind, and then, I am suddenly jolted back to the reality that I can never call her again ... not in this lifetime. I still grieve over that loss, and also I accept that she is gone.

In our house, we talk about her all the time. My children adored her and have some wonderful memories of her. She was an avid collector of Coca-Cola collectibles, and every time I pass a Coca-Cola truck on the road, I smile and tell her I love her. Although I have accepted her death, it doesn't mean that I don't miss her. It doesn't mean I suppress my emotions. And so, sometimes, I cry when I am looking at the baby-blue sky remembering that was her favorite color. I ride the wave of emotions, feel the love I still have for my mom, and smile in gratitude for having had a mom who loved me.

Nonjudgmental: Another cornerstone skill I learned in dialectical behavior therapy was learning to think and act nonjudgmentally. In fact, I didn't realize how often I was judging myself and everyone around me. Did you know the human mind is wired to judge? Unless we notice and change the behavior, it can become a negative habit that causes unhappiness.

Judging reflexively causes unhappiness within us and also projects it out to those around us. We've all been there, shopping at the local Target where we witness someone's kid throwing a tantrum while we throw judgment on the parenting in play. Or when we dislike someone's style and call it ugly or disapprove of someone else's choices of tattoos—as if we have the right to disapprove of anyone to begin with.

It comes down to accepting that we are all human and we are all different. And yet, we are still the same. We have different tastes and lifestyles and preferences. We have different values, and we, for damn sure, ALL sin the same as everyone around us, even if in different ways. We all have our own internal demons that we struggle with, though some of us cover them up better than others. Judging and gossiping about other people's choices only lowers our self-respect and our value.

Inner Child Work and Inner Rebel

Love Your Inner Child

We must heal, nurture, and honor our inner child. I know some people aren't aware of what this means and some believe it's hokey pokey stuff. However, I assure you that it's a real thing. Just like we all have an ego, we all have an inner child (and inner rebel too). And our upbringing and childhood trauma determines how much healing we need. Our inner child needs to feel seen, heard, validated, and safe. If we have any ignored trauma, our inner child can and will find a way to protect us and be seen. Such protection is similar to that of our subconscious mind, so while the intention is good, it more often than not does more damage. It doesn't matter if you were raised in the perfect Mary Poppins household, we all have something to deal with and our inner child needs to be nourished.

Even with limited or healed past trauma, our inner child likes to come out and play sometimes. Those activities are unique to each individual, and should we choose not to nurture our inner child, our inner rebel will take over, creating sabotage and problems.

Ways to love our inner child include

- Talking to a therapist
- Talking to your inner child, ask them questions
- Acknowledging your inner child. Notice their triggers.
- Revisiting positive childhood memories
- Journaling
- Doing activities you enjoyed as a child such as coloring, playing video games, playing sports, doing arts and crafts
- Being creative
- Having a lazy day, being messy, having dessert for dinner
- Spending time with children
- Reading a favorite childhood book
- Dancing around the house
- Eating your favorite cereal from when you were a child
- Talking to an old friend from childhood

If we do not allow our inner child to feel seen, heard, and validated, it can then become rebellious and have a tantrum, just like a child. We may scream, pout, slam doors, or—even worse—abuse drugs or other substances. We may manipulate others, lie, and even cheat. Our inner rebel can cause havoc. Sometimes, we have to nurture that side of us, too, in order to remain balanced. After all, we can't be good all the time.

Ways to nurture our inner rebel include

- Removing the DO NOT REMOVE tag from the mattress

- Playing hooky
- Prank calling a friend
- Dyeing hair a crazy color or wearing a fun wig for the day
- Creating an alter ego and playing in character
- Having sex anywhere BUT the bed, maybe even outside or in front of an open window (anything illegal is at your own discretion, and watch out for children)
- Removing your mouth filter for one hour
- Talking about an edgy or racy subject

Believe in the Reasons

If I were to give examples of every ingredient in my recipe for happiness, this chapter would never end. But I firmly believe that everything happens for a reason. Life is not fair by any means, and so many times, we are left pondering why any God would allow such things to happen. Without getting too spiritual or religious, I believe that sometimes we have to go through painful, unjust experiences for certain internal lessons to be learned or to ignite something within ourselves or maybe to spark something within another person ... even years after the experience. Maybe a trauma can ignite passion for a cause to help others or to start a passionate career or hobby. Or maybe to write a book that can make a little bit of difference in the world. We wouldn't have the writings of Anne Frank had she not initially set the intention to write a diary as a young teenager while living through one of the scariest and most traumatic times in human history.

Why do we humans focus so much on all the bad things and suppress so many happy, positive memories? Why do so many become addicted to suffering and to being a victim? Did you know it takes five to seven positive thoughts to outweigh one negative?

I didn't come from happiest of childhoods. I wasn't raised by securely attached parents or even within a securely attached family. I had to learn better and healthier coping skills on my own through years of trial and error, of therapy and reflection. I had to come to terms with the fact that I could choose to be miserable and continue with the family dysfunction I was raised in or choose to make a change—to choose to be happy regardless of my past. Regardless of my childhood and regardless of my adult mistakes.

I am by no means perfect, and I will forever be a work in progress. But I will be damned if I continue this family cycle and allow it to trickle into my children's lives, leading them to live lives of misery. I strive to break these family cycles, or family curses, as some call them.

8

Find Your Self-Worth

> ***Self-worth:*** *an individual's evaluation of himself or herself as a valuable, capable human being deserving of respect and consideration. Positive feelings of self-worth tend to be associated with a high degree of self-acceptance and self-esteem.*
>
> American Psychological Association

We determine and enable how others treat us. Read that again. That's a statement that a lot of people don't understand. They really don't want to even hear it. Of course, you can't control what other people do. But you can control how you respond and what you accept. *How so?* you ask. Let me start with this. If you're at a store and another customer is harassing you or yelling at you, what do you do? You stand up for yourself. You walk away. You go tell a manager or whatever you need to do, but you don't tolerate it. You either enable the harassment or you stop it from happening.

Same thing goes with people who are closer to us. Our partners, our friends, our parents, our siblings. If these people continually hurt us, that becomes our fault too. As adults, we have accountability and responsibility in every situation in our life. Even the spouse who is at home being physically beaten or mentally abused by their partner still has some degree of responsibility in that situation. By choosing to stay. By choosing to tolerate it. By choosing to allow it to keep happening. Thus, enabling it. It doesn't matter what the reasons are; it is still a choice. It doesn't matter the justifications. At the end of the day, the individual on the receiving end of the abuse is still allowing it to happen. And they do this because of low self-esteem or self-worth. A shrinking perspective on the extent of their own value becomes their home.

Our judgments against the spouse who stays isn't helpful either because, even though we all have a choice, there is deep-seated subconscious shit going on, making it not so simple.

I once knew a woman who tried to control everything her husband did. From day one, she gave him a weekly monetary allowance to stop him from smoking cigarettes and drinking. He wasn't allowed to hang out with his friends unless she was with him. He chose to stay for years as he snuck around town bumming cigarettes from friends and family, and sneaking in a drink here and there. Her illusion of controlling her husband is a reflection of her internal self-worth. The same is true of his decision to tolerate that abusive behavior.

Tolerate: *allow the existence, occurrence, or practice of (something that one does not necessarily like or agree with) without interference*

—Oxford Dictionary (Google)

As adults, we decide how others treat us. No, we can't control what other people do. We can't stop anyone from doing anything. But what we can do is set limits on how we let the impact of their actions land on us. Instead of protecting ourselves, many of us enable bad behavior simply by putting up with it. We do not enforce our own boundaries, which leads to continued poor treatment, followed by resentment of the perpetrator, followed by unhappiness.

Many years ago, I planned a huge birthday party for my now ex-husband. I planned that thing for months and kept it on the down-low until a week or two before the exciting day. In perfect "Stepford-like" fashion, I had the guests and a guest of honor, the DJ, the photographer, the entertainment, the decorations, the dress, and the hair. The cake was customized to replicate the rims of his own personal car that he so loved at the time. A lot of love and effort went into this party for him.

Close to a hundred people filled our home, including his work colleagues and family. Throughout the evening, my husband floated around the house talking to everyone ... except his wife. At one point, he walked right past me, deliberately ignoring me. He spent the evening staying really close to another woman, who he actually started to open presents with. He didn't include me until I inserted myself.

I was so confused about the whole evening. I felt invisible and so unappreciated and undervalued—and by the one person whose duty it was to always make sure HE saw me. A couple of days later, while I was at my computer typing up a test for our middle school child who I was homeschooling at the time, my spouse sat at a nearby desk talking about the party for the first time. Instead of expressing gratitude and appreciation toward me for the party, he proceeded to talk about how amazing that woman was, the one he'd lavished his attention on at the party. Over and over again, he said, "She's so amazing! Simply amazing."

Although his behavior was hurtful to me, I wasn't especially threatened by this woman because I was thinking that regardless of what he may have thought about her, she was too classy for him. Yet looking back, I could have held myself to a higher standard than I did by way of comparison. I kept staring at the computer screen, with my back to him as he carried on about her many attributes. I felt so hurt and insecure and inferior, even as he listed off the same qualities I knew I had. I felt such pain in my heart as I listened to the man I loved brag gratuitously about another woman, all while ignoring me and disregarding my feelings. Of course, it turned into a huge fight, one that was never resolved. I left him almost exactly a year later.

It brought me back to when I was a little girl . . . when nobody heard me crying for help after I was sexually abused. I felt unseen. I felt invisible. I felt unimportant to the adults I relied on to protect me. And now I felt the same way with my own husband.

I was molested by three additional men from that point on, until I was thirteen. I never told anyone about these other three men until I was an adult. I felt ashamed. I felt embarrassed. I felt dirty. I felt responsible.

And I felt that I wasn't going to be heard anyway, so why bother telling? Even if someone were to hear what I had to say, they wouldn't help me. So I put walls up around myself and tried to stay invisible, and the abuse continued.

There is a little girl inside me who feels scared, abandoned, and uncertain about whom she can trust. She feels alone, deserted by both of her parents. She feels emotionally cast off by many people in her life. Every time her grandmother invalidates and belittles her past struggles, she feels unseen. Every time she thinks back about the men who touched her in places they had no right touching, she feels dirty and ashamed. She feels unheard. Nobody believes her.

The sight of those men made my stomach turn. I remember one evening when I was lying in bed and I couldn't find my special blanket, which was literally my security blanket. My mom and her "friends" were in the living room watching TV as I looked around for it. It just so happened that the abuser was sitting on my blanket. I remember feeling disgusted when he handed it to me. Needless to say, I didn't hold on to my blanket that night, and it had to be washed. Anyone who has ever had a security blanket or stuffed animal understands that washing makes the "good smell" go away. But his smell and his energy had to go.

One of those abusers had a smell that haunted me for thirty years. Any time I accidentally inhaled a whiff of what I later learned was patchouli, I felt revulsion. So many times, I would walk past someone who smelled like him and I would stop inhaling mid-breath until I sensed the odor was gone. Flashbacks of the horrific experience I'd had would flood my senses, and the shame would ripple over me. Sometimes I was able to shake the flashbacks, while other times I would spend longer periods ruminating and feeling disgust. Fast-forward to today: while patchouli is still repulsive to me, I am not jolted back in time the way I used to be. I still hold my breath, but now it is a memory that comes and quickly goes.

I chose to stay in an unhappy marriage and add to the dysfunction because I subconsciously thought that was love. Until I decided it wasn't, and I was going to validate and see my own self-worth.

Either Way, It's a Choice

When we're with a partner who doesn't share our values or a partner who doesn't respect our boundaries, and we continue to stay with that partner, we are agreeing to what happens. We are enabling it to happen. And we are only adding more toxic fuel and more poison to the relationship because resentment builds up, further inflaming the situation.

Sometimes we have to walk away from people whom we love very much because they are hurting us. Sometimes the hurt they inflict is not directly aimed at us, but watching our loved ones relentlessly hurt themselves is painful to us, and we have to walk away. Other times, someone we love is hurting us directly, and then we really have to walk away. If we love ourselves and know our worth, we will not put up with emotional, physical, or mental abuse—*from anybody*. And the longer we stay with such a partner or hang around people who treat us like that, the more we ensure it is going to continue to happen.

Humans are habitual creatures. They love habits. If someone close to us has a habit of taking advantage of us or walking all over us because we allow it to happen, they are not going to stop doing it. It's up to us to stop it. We can try to fix relationships with therapy or coaches. We can try all kinds of stuff, and I'm all for that. Sometimes, it's not enough. Sometimes, you try and you try and you do everything you think you're capable of. And still, there is a choice to be made.

One choice is to stay and continue in that relationship or situation that doesn't make you happy and is leading to suffering. Remember, bad shit happens to all of us, but suffering is a choice. Sometimes, the choice to walk away is the hardest thing—the most painful thing—you have to do, and yet it's the only way you can be happy again within yourself. Because the other person is not going to change, not until *they're* ready to change.

We must value ourselves in order for others to value us. If we think lowly of ourselves, we will act that way, and other people will think lowly of us too, including those we love. I know a woman who has this belief that you cannot meet a decent partner in a bar. From her experiences and what she's witnessed with others, including her own children, none of them have met worthy people at a bar. And they haven't. What she doesn't seem to understand is that like attracts like. A person who values themself highly (a high-value person) can walk into a bar and meet another such person. A person with low self-esteem (a low-value person) will go into the same bar and attract a person who lives with the same poor self-estimation.

Energy speaks volumes. A high-value person typically won't even approach a low-value person. You can tell when you walk into that bar who are the low-value people and the high-value people by the energy they project. Low-value people act in different ways than do high-value people. They talk in different tones. They sit differently and project different attitudes. They speak different words. They express different *everything*. A high-value person acts in ways that attract other high-value people, and there is mutual recognition. It would be no different on the job or at a bookstore.

My past does not define my future. I came from a lower middle-class family. I came from a broken home. I was in the foster care system, and I lived in a group home for half of my junior year of high school. I am divorced. I've been cheated on, and I've cheated. I've been sexually violated. I have stirred the pot and caused drama where there wasn't any during some dark times in my life. That does not mean that I am nothing. That does not mean that I have no worth.

Those are snapshots of my life, and what it means is that I have scars, battle wounds from this thing called life. A lot of bad shit happened to me. And no, I'm not perfect. But that doesn't mean I'm a bad person. It doesn't mean I'm broken or damaged goods. It simply means I am human. We all have our own sins and our own baggage. Now, it's my choice of whether to fall prey to feeling like a victim or to be someone who knows her worth and owns her power.

Know Your Worth, and Add Tax

We have to learn to love ourselves. We have to learn to not judge ourselves. We have to learn to forgive ourselves. The more we love ourselves, the less bullshit we will put up with from other people. People can love us only as much as we love ourselves. People can treat us only the way we allow them to treat us. We may not like the choices that we have. Leaving a relationship, or even a family dynamic, is sometimes the only option left in making room for our intrinsic happiness. Sometimes we have to raise our standards, lower our expectations, and move the heck on.

One of the easiest ways to begin loving ourselves is to talk to ourselves differently. Humans have a negative mindset by default. We naturally judge ourselves and others, and it's up to us to acknowledge that and change those habits. These are automatic negative thoughts that creep into our story and make us who we are.

Try this: look at your reflection and notice the first five thoughts that come to your head. Are they negative thoughts? Are you judging your hair, the wrinkles on your face? Do your thoughts center on your nose? Instead, look in the mirror and give yourself a positive affirmation. Tell yourself you're beautiful or you're amazing or just tell yourself anything your heart desires. Throughout the day, try to observe and notice the thoughts going through your mind. Don't judge them, just observe them. When you're ready, try changing them to positive thoughts.

Did you know that studies show it takes five positive affirmations or comments to erase one negative thought? It wasn't until I was in DBT that I fully came to understand what being judgmental is and how often I was doing it. Just think about it and be honest with yourself about how judgmental you really are. When you're at the store and you're watching the mother with a screaming child who she can't get under control at that moment in time, what thoughts float into your head? What about when you see an overweight person? What do you think when you see somebody with face piercings? What do you think when you see somebody with more kids than they should have—in your opinion? All these negative thoughts are constantly running through our minds over and over and over, which then creates a negative mindset.

Like attracts like. Therefore, negative thoughts will draw in more negative thoughts, which then creates a negative mood that bleeds into every other part of our lives, including our self-worth. The negative things we say about others is nothing more than a reflection of what we're thinking and feeling about ourselves. Think about what you say to yourself or tell yourself on a constant basis. *I'm fat, I'm ugly, my hair is frizzy, my complexion is blotchy, my cottage-cheese legs are ugly, my boobs are too small.* Or you may fling other insults at yourself like *what an idiot I am!* or *how stupid could I have been?* or *nobody will love me.*

One of the pillars of DBT is mindfulness, and one of the skills of mindfulness is observing. Simply observing, without judgment. It's been one of my favorite skills I've learned so far. There are some others as well, but I found it quite fascinating to discover just how negative I was all those years ago.

To observe your thoughts without judgment, you have to first notice and acknowledge the judgments without judging the thought itself. After all, we are human, and we're still learning. For instance, you see a woman wearing an outfit you don't care for, and your first thought is *what an ugly style. Ugly* is definitely a judgment because it's an opinion. She clearly likes what she's wearing, and either way, it is a negative thought, which draws in more negativity.

I have learned that when I notice I am judging or saying something negative about somebody else in my head, I can counteract it with three positive observations about that same person. For example, there was the lady at Target with the screaming child (who I was feeling free to judge, even knowing that we've all been there). I would compliment the woman in my mind by thinking, *She's doing the best she can in this moment, and the color blue she's wearing looks really pretty with her skin tone, and remember, this moment is just a snapshot in her life.* Another skill I learned and love, and still do to this day, is to genuinely compliment three people.

With simple things like changing my choice of language and the tone of my inner dialogue, I soon started feeling better about myself. I used to look in the mirror and judge every flaw I could find about my face and body, but today, I feel the most beautiful I've felt in my entire life. I tell myself I am beautiful, and I embrace my physical scars and imperfections. I used to believe that kind of embrace of self-love made a person conceited or narcissistic. But what it means, quite simply, is that I value myself and my worth.

Another thing we can do to raise our sense of self-worth is to remember other people's opinions and judgments about snapshot moments in our lives and the purported mistakes we've made are nobody's business but *theirs*. They are, of course, entitled to their opinions and judgments. But they do not determine how I feel about myself. Nobody is perfect. Nobody is sinless. And I do not choose to spend my energy concerned about what other people think of me.

People pleasing, trying to "keep up with the Joneses," allowing never-ending distractions, neglecting self-care—all of these things create low self-worth and self-value within.

Letting Go of the Misery-Loves-Company Crowd

Look at the people around you. Think of the people that you hang out with and interact with on a regular basis. There's a high probability that the five people who are closest to you are very similar to you. That could be a good thing. However, if the five people you hang out with are lazy, unmotivated, negative, and play the victim card, then that could be not such a good thing. There's a high probability, like a 99.9 percent chance, that you are pretty much the same.

There was a time when I hung around a large group of low-value individuals. They were highly negative, highly critical, toxic people. They were two-faced and just mean. When I was around them, I never felt good; actually, I felt miserable inside. I felt beat down. I felt bullied. I felt like I was a punching bag for them as they criticized and judged everything about me and anyone else they came in contact with. I didn't know what I know now, and I am not a part of that group any longer. But back when I was, I didn't think I had a choice but to tolerate them ... until I chose to leave.

I can honestly look back and feel bad for them because they are only reflecting how miserable they feel on the inside. They have to put others down to make themselves feel better. Make others feel stupid to make themselves feel smart. Since walking away from that horrible clique, I have finally found my self-worth. I do not expect perfection, nor do I expect people not to make mistakes. But I will not continually put up with people who use me, abuse me, manipulate me, lie to me, or do anything else that will hurt me.

Immersing ourselves in an environment filled with positive people and positive influences is another way to build up our self-worth. Sometimes, that means letting go of our best friend, who only brings us down or wants to be a part of our lives only when it's convenient. Sometimes, we have to step up our game and walk away, knowing at an intrinsic level that we are amazing.

Do what makes you happy.

You hear people say "be yourself," only for society then to judge us because who we happen to be is not to their preference. If we all liked the same things and had the same opinions and the same beliefs, needs, and wants, we'd be robots. So rock that pink hair, rock Taylor Swift, own your values, and *be yourself.* There are seven billion people in this world—not everyone is going to like us anyway.

9

Therapies and Coaching

Your relationship with yourself is the foundation of every relationship you have in life.

Mel Robbins

We all need help sometimes. Invest in yourself because nobody else will. Whether or not we have the money we need, we all have the time to invest in our own intrinsic value.

It is my honest opinion that everyone on this planet has their own shit to deal with and that we all could benefit from therapy from time to time. Sometimes, even therapists need therapists. I also firmly believe that we could all make good use of coaches and mentors, even coaches themselves. I consider Tony Robbins my virtual dad and mentor. He's one of the best in the world of personal development, and even he has a team of coaches.

And for those of you thinking you don't need a coach because you have accomplished so much intrinsically and externally, good for you. Now imagine how much further you could go with your own cheerleader or drill sergeant stretching your potential. Research where Tony started and where he is now. He does not have a college degree. He has twenty-four hours in his day, just like the rest of us, while he cares for himself and multiple businesses—around thirty or so—and he has a happy and successful marriage. He is one of the leaders in personal development, and *he* uses coaching.

Therapy and coaching are part of our mental health system, and with that comes the stigma attached to it. So many people refuse therapy and coaching because they view it as a sign of weakness, when in reality, reaching out when needed is a sign of great strength. The weakness lies in NOT improving ourselves. The weakness lies in living life on autopilot and not facing those inner demons. We all have them, whether we admit them or not. It doesn't matter if you come from the most loving, stable home or have a healthy marriage. We all have something we battle internally and we all have areas in our lives to improve. Believing otherwise reveals a stagnant mindset.

As far as coaching is concerned, not only can this process help us improve on our inner weaknesses and relieve us of our demons, but also stretch our potential in any area we choose. If you have a successful business right now or you live a healthy lifestyle, imagine how much further you could go with the individual motivation directed your way from a coach.

Writing It Out

I received my first journal from my best friend after middle school graduation. The journal was padded with a jewel-toned mandala pattern on both sides. I no longer have that journal as I went through a purging phase and threw it away when I moved into my first apartment. I wish I hadn't done that. All I have left from that journal is a sheet of paper I ripped out of it with a handwritten poem I wrote that was published a long time ago. I copied out the only part of the Serenity Prayer I knew on the first page, and then I started writing.

I remember sitting on my daybed in my bedroom at my grandparents' apartment, looking out the window that overlooked a busy road and writing in that book all the time. I had bubble handwriting that still emerges every once in a while as I write. I would write about teenage problems and my inner struggles that seem so silly now but still feel intense when I think back. I rarely go back and read my journals. But when I do, I am often amazed at how far I have come and how much I have learned and grown.

Regular journaling has been scientifically proven to help reduce anxiety and depression (the two leading mental disorders in the world). It can help us overcome trauma and even improve memory function. It gives us a safe place to be honest about our thoughts and feelings, and certainly a way to try to understand them. Journals or diaries are a sacred space that should never be intruded upon by anyone. Anyone who reads someone else's journal without the express permission of the writer is invading privacy and breaching trust.

Therapies

Couples Therapy

Unfortunately, this type of therapy gets a bad reputation. So many people believe couples therapy doesn't work because, more often than not, it doesn't. But that says less about the efficacy of the therapy than the fact that typically couples wait, on average, through six years of unhappiness before seeking external treatment. By the time a couple enters therapy, it is usually too late. However, entering therapy sooner improves the chances it will be successful.

Premarital Counseling and Couples Coaching

For those of us who have an insecure attachment style, we will always come up short in our relationships. Coaching and therapy early on can help us develop skills and new habits to create a harmonious and happy relationship.

Talk Therapy

Most of my therapy has involved talk therapy. Like journaling, the more consistent you are with it, the more helpful it becomes. Not all therapists are equal, and they all have their own methods of practice.

Sometimes, we may not jive with a particular therapist, and that is 100 percent okay. Find another one. Keep looking, if needed, until you find one that fits your budget and fits your personality. And remember, therapy doesn't have to be forever.

You may find this process hard at times as repressed feelings and memories can resurface, but that is a good thing. As mentally exhausting as the therapeutic process can be, it is worth the effort. Emotions we are not even aware of that haunt us at a subconscious level can be released through effective therapy.

Rapid Resolution Therapy (RRT)

What I love about RRT is that it's intense but fast. Sessions typically run three hours at a time, but the overall duration is short—typically two to eight sessions are all that is needed. RRT uses guided imagery, hypnosis, stories, and other forms of communication to resolve our negative and troubling thoughts, behaviors, and emotions. It is often used to help those suffering from PTSD (post-traumatic stress disorder) and c-PTSD (complex post-traumatic stress disorder).

Post-traumatic stress disorder (PTSD): *a psychiatric disorder that may occur in people who have experienced or witnessed a traumatic event such as a natural disaster, a serious accident, a terrorist act, war/combat, or rape or who have been threatened with death, sexual violence, or serious injury.*

—American Psychiatric Association

Complex post-traumatic stress disorder (c-PTSD): *In some cases (of PTSD) people experience chronic trauma that continues or repeats for months or years at a time. Some have suggested that the current PTSD diagnosis does not fully capture the severe psychological harm that occurs with prolonged, repeated trauma.*

—National Center for PTSD (U.S. Department of Veterans Affairs)

I used RRT to help me forgive my mom and my ex-husband. My first session was focused mostly on my relationship with my mom. My therapist did some exercises with me that would help me control my anxiety around my mom and not be so angry with her. I remember, after the first session, driving home thinking it wasn't going to work. However, when I arrived home, where she was waiting with my children, I immediately noticed that I was not defensive upon seeing her.

In spite of my anger toward my mom, I really wasn't all that mean to her. But when I was with her, I felt lots of emotions that sometimes caused me to just go quiet. I honestly didn't want to hurt her feelings as that was something I couldn't stand. Seeing her cry was always a hard thing for me, and if it were ever me that made her cry, the guilt would rush over me immediately. As infuriated as I was for her past mistakes, it was hard for me to show her my anger because she was, in fact, a different person than she had been when I was a child. So this inner conflict was a challenge. RRT really helped me deal with my emotions and forgive my mom, and I am forever grateful.

Dialectical Behavior Therapy (DBT)

DBT is a form of CBT (cognitive behavior therapy). One of my psychologists described DBT as "CBT on steroids." It was created and developed by Marsha Linehan in the seventies after her experience with being institutionalized for schizophrenia and borderline personality disorder. The schizophrenia was a misdiagnosis, and her BPD is now managed effectively using her methods, without medication.

DBT can help a person create a balanced life, deal with stress, and improve relationships. A lot of the skills mentioned in this book are personal favorites drawn from this method of therapy. I have learned the most from DBT, and I have thought about doing it again just to sharpen up and learn new skills.

I firmly believe that DBT could be highly effective among society at large if it were implemented in our school systems. DBT can help with ADHD, generalized anxiety disorder, bipolar, PTSD, and even OCD. There is a focus on dealing with addiction, too, which I used a few times in dealing with my shopping and spending habits.

Most of the skills we rely on day to day are the ones we are taught at home. Yet our caregiver's skills may not always be healthy or effective for us. For that reason, we can all benefit from learning new skills to get us through life. DBT is often done in a group setting for several reasons: it comforts us to know we are not alone and it helps us practice the new skills we are learning with each other. This group process can be intimidating, at first, but worthwhile.

Dialectical basically means seeing both sides of a situation. *Our loved ones can hurt us AND love us.* "And" is an important part of DBT because, as a conjunction that brings two or more ideas together, it helps us understand that two sides can be right and wrong simultaneously. It helps eliminate the black-and-white thinking that so many humans adopt without even realizing it.

DBT tells us it is possible for these statements to be true: "I am disappointed in you AND I still love you," "I understand your point of view AND I can still disagree with you." (I sure wish this were a standard used in politics.) It helps us learn to balance our emotions and logic and to think wisely, or in what is referred to as *wise mind*. It's about learning the following:

pain + resistance = suffering

There are four modules or pillars in DBT. Each offers dozens of skills we can pick from and add into our "toolbox" of life skills.

- **Mindfulness (the core):** Mindfulness is the core of all the pillars, for without it, the other pillars are nonexistent. It focuses on *awareness*, *breathing*, and *meditation*. It teaches us to notice our judgments AND learn from them. It draws out our curiosity and understanding of ourselves and others. It helps develop patience, trust, and acceptance. Example skill: Noticing Thoughts Nonjudgmentally
- **Emotion Regulation:** This one is pretty self-explanatory. It not only helps us understand emotions in general, it helps us understand OUR OWN emotions and triggers, along with ways to regulate them while getting our needs met and

without causing additional suffering. It teaches us the skills to control our emotions and mental state such as taking the opposite action of how we are feeling, like listening to upbeat music when we're sad. Example skill: Opposite Action

- **Distress Tolerance:** Sometimes when certain situations arise, our emotions get the best of us, and we can go down a path of actions that lead to regret and repair. This module, or pillar, teaches us skills to step back from stressful situations. Example skill: Self-Soothing
- **Interpersonal Effectiveness:** This module, in my opinion, is the most challenging. It teaches us how to communicate with ourselves and other people in our lives. It teaches us skills to express ourselves in a healthy manner AND hear the other party as well. We learn to ask for what we want, learn to say no, and maintain boundaries. It helps us see both sides, and it helps our relationships with others. Example skill: Validation

Neurofeedback

I believe neurofeedback (NFB) is the most underrated and underused therapy out there. Going back to my previous chapter on our failing mental health system, this therapy is not covered by insurance, and it really should be. I stumbled across this form of treatment while researching non-drug solutions for ADHD. Twenty sessions and $3,000 later, my child no longer showed signs of ADHD and no longer required any medication or therapy.

Throughout my many hours spent with the doctor during my son's treatment, I learned about all the things neurofeedback can help with, so I decided to use it to cure my bipolar disorder. I remember him trying to explain to me how the programming works and that treating me for a condition I didn't have was going to be a waste of time. After about ten to fifteen sessions with zero improvement, I finally listened to him and started treatment for trauma.

That was the last form of treatment I underwent before finding my first and favorite life coach, Alma. This doctor was the one who later helped me find a qualified and trusted MD to wean me off my medications for a disorder I never had.

Yoga

While many believe yoga is just a physical practice, it is way deeper than that. Yoga has great physical properties such as contributing to development of a lean and flexible body, but it also heals us physically, mentally, emotionally, and spiritually. Yoga is more than movement; it is a mindset and an internal belief system that promotes balance and harmony within us.

Self-Help Resources

Online Printable Mini Courses

Of course, not everyone can afford to pay out of pocket for every type of therapy, and it can be expensive. After my divorce, as I was learning to budget my finances, I was paying around $500 a month in therapy, not including my medications. The balancing of resources required to obtain the treatment you need with what you can afford financially can be stressful and challenging. However, there is a world of digital downloads and mini courses available for sale online that I have found incredibly useful tools for therapy. The DailyOM and Etsy are a couple of sources. They start under $20, and it's so convenient and wonderful to have all of the world's knowledge and experiences at our fingertips.

Self-Help Books and eBooks

I have always loved books, and I enjoy reading both fiction and nonfiction. My favorite way to read nonfiction is by listening to the books being read. Several times a week, I listen to audio of my personal development books while I am driving, when I go for a walk or a run, or even by using my AirPods to listen while blow-drying my hair. I often purchase the book itself as well, so I can reference back and forth. It has really been a game changer in my growth.

My favorite books that I read and listen to yearly are *The Four Agreements* by Don Miguel Ruiz and *Think and Grow Rich* by Napoleon Hill. Those two are staples in my life. Another favorite book that I have purchased as gifts for so many is *The Boy, The Mole, The Fox, and The Horse* by Charlie Mackesy. It is a book for all ages that can be read in fifteen minutes, and while it's not really a self-help book, I find so many valuable lessons and so much wisdom in that book. I cry and feel emotions upon reading different pages each time I return to it. Good emotions. Gratitude fills me up every single time I read this book, which happens to be a lot.

Seminars and Webinars

My first self-help seminar was a Tony Robbins event in Miami called Unleash the Power Within (UPW). It was three days, in person, and I took my oldest son with me. Those three days were packed with so much information from so many different people in the personal development world. One of my favorite things I learned was making use of body movement. "Shake your booty" and move it! It may not make any of your problems go away, but it can, in fact, improve the moment and your current mindset, which then helps with your problems. Improving the Moment is also a skill in the DBT distress tolerance module discussed earlier.

YouTube

YouTube has become my ultimate form of social media. I use it every single day starting in the morning with guided meditations and motivational montages from some of the best experts out there on intrinsic happiness, confidence, and success—Oprah Winfrey, Tony of course, Jim Rohn, Bob Proctor, Mel Robbins, and Les Brown, to name a few.

Years ago, when I first started watching YouTube, I was learning about attachment styles, and this man with a raspy voice kept interrupting with his commercials. I would roll my eyes because commercials annoy me, and his voice really bothered me. I would wait the minimum amount of time and hit the X button to get back on with my video. One day, I listened to the whole commercial, which was actually an ad for Tony Robbins's Netflix show *I Am Not Your Guru*. It was a blast of inspiration, and I watched the Netflix show immediately. I have been a Tony fan ever since, and now when I hear his voice, I am attentive and motivated.

I have since started paying for YouTube so I no longer have to "suffer" through the commercials. But had I not watched that one, I wouldn't have watched that show and I wouldn't have attended UPW and I wouldn't have met one of my current coaches, who also happens to lead a mastermind group that I am starting my third year with. In fact, she had an intervention with Tony Robbins at one his events many years ago before she became the brilliant and compassionate coach she is today.

A Tony intervention is when he selects participants at his live events and helps them break through their limiting beliefs. He is gentle but direct and doesn't allow space for excuses. Seeing my coach's intervention and knowing the person she is today inspires me more than words can describe.

At the end of the day, it takes a lot of strength and courage to face our internal demons, fears, and shortcomings. It takes a certain amount of self-awareness to notice what our weaknesses are and surround ourselves with a tribe or support network that helps us become better versions of ourselves.

Meditation

Meditation is a simple, yet tricky, skill to learn that in itself has nothing to with religion or spirituality ... unless you want it to and choose to incorporate that focus into your practice. Our brains and minds never stop. Giving our minds even a few minutes of stillness and calmness to not think so much each day has been scientifically proven to reduce stress and anxiety and to help control our emotions.

Breathwork is intentionally changing the way we breathe. As our emotions change, our breathing changes. When we are triggered or upset, we breathe more heavily, which can lead us into a panic attack. When we are depressed, our breathing is shallower. By intentionally changing our breathing patterns, we can effectively change our emotions. While this won't fix all our problems, it does improve the moment (a DBT skill in the emotion regulation module) and allows us to better control ourselves. Breathwork is used in yoga as well. The internet is filled with information on this topic.

For those of us who have difficulty with sitting meditations, there are mindful moving meditations we can do. There are walking meditations, and I personally enjoy meditating during yoga. Doing this practice daily and focusing on our breath helps us be more at peace. And if we are alive, we all have our breath, and it's always FREE.

Life and Health Coaches

Of course, I am biased toward coaching. I am a coach, and I use a team of coaches myself. I still use my original coach, who is an angel. She helped me with my anxiety, and she helped me learn to eat healthier without dieting. She always has guided me toward my own goals, no matter what they were and no matter how she felt about them. When I first started using Alma, I had a goal of putting my family of five back together. She supported that goal and helped me in so many ways. When I decided to not put my family back together and instead to focus on my children and myself, she was elated. She said that was the best goal I had made thus far.

I remember asking her why she never said anything, and her response was, "It's not my place to tell you what I think you should do. My job is to help you accomplish your goals." I am forever grateful that she allowed me to go through the motions and figure it out on my own. When I arrived at that point, it was, in fact, one of the best decisions of my life.

Coaches are like therapists in that they have their own niches and experiences. Not all coaches are equal, and they have many methods they use. Most coaches choose a niche that they have explicit experience with, whether it's weight loss, anxiety, career, self-esteem, time management, relationships, or another area. It is my personal opinion that you cannot fully teach or coach what you haven't experienced. Many therapists, psychologists, and psychiatrists have a lot of book knowledge about mental health but limited experience with most of it. How can anyone truly empathize with a person who is going through something they have never experienced?

I have used spiritual coaches, time-management coaches, business coaches, a sex coach, and even an INFJ (Myers-Briggs) coach who works only with other INFJs, and multiple relationship coaches. I am obsessed with personal development and human behavior, and I am passionate about coaching. I feel I have grown the most with coaching, far more than I ever have with talk therapy.

I needed therapy at one time and I may need it again in the future. But my coaches keep me accountable, hold me to my own standards, and call me out on my shit. I pay them money to help me grow the way I want to and find my own happiness. Sometimes I am triggered by their call-outs as my fight or flight instincts kick in, and I want to hang up the call. However, I remind myself that the trigger is there for a reason, and that it is an area to focus on and grow from. I have not hung up on a coach yet.

As a coach myself, my niche is *self-love*. I am a relationship coach specializing in self-love for moms. All moms—stay-at-home moms, divorced moms, single moms, step moms, etc. I focus on the relationship with themselves and with their partner. I help teach skills to successfully co-parent. As a mom of three for almost twenty years, I have plenty of experience. I can help with many areas, including healthy lifestyle and better sleep. As you may discover, along with finding intrinsic happiness comes a side-effect—organically improving all areas of our lives.

One of my clients felt stuck at her job. She'd stayed with it for over a decade, and she was miserable. After working with me for less than a year, she found the courage to get a new job, and now she couldn't be happier.

She had been working in an office setting surrounded by negative individuals who put her in a bad mood daily. I helped her change her mindset and learn to not take things from her coworkers so personally. I helped her understand that her negative coworkers were just projecting their internal unhappiness. She was able to make the last six months of that position more tolerable as she began to understand herself and others better, adopting compassion for her negative coworkers instead of resentment.

While a new job was what she wanted, stepping outside of her comfort zone was the next step in that direction. While she was working on herself, we took baby steps toward finding her internal self-worth in the workplace, starting with breaking out the ten-year-old resume and updating it. That exercise alone boosted so much of the confidence she had lost.

I approach my coaching by meeting my clients exactly where they are at that moment. I do not lead them down any path but their own. I simply have the questions that lead them to THEIR answers. I take a slow and gentle approach but can also be assertive if and when it is needed.

If you think you may be interested in working with a life and health coach who can help you make your best effort toward achieving whatever goals matter most to you, visit my website at www.jenslifecoaching.com.

Conclusion

The expert in anything was once a beginner.

Helen Hayes

Holy cow! I am finally writing the conclusion of my very first book! Congratulations to me and congratulations to you for getting this far. I am definitely giving myself a high five for this accomplishment. I am trying to focus here, but all I feel is giddiness because I am so happy. I am so freaking proud of myself. Tears are welling up as I feel not only pride, but sadness that my parents could not see this day. My spiritual side reminds me that they do see me and they have both been a part of every single word I have typed for this book. Their picture is in the same spot as it was when I started this journey, on the corkboard to the left of my laptop. Their love and support during this exploration has been uncanny as I literally feel them with me. I know they are proud of me wherever their souls are resting. I know I have broken off a link in this chain of familial self-destruction.

Happiness is our birthright. Every single one of us is entitled to be happy. It is also our decision and responsibility to be happy, nobody else's. When we rely on ONLY external factors to create happiness for ourselves, we are chasing nothing more than a carrot on a stick that we will never catch. Our careers and families and friends are a part of us, and they can all bring joy. They can all bring misery as well. But our true happiness comes from within. There is absolutely no other way.

As with everything new, we start. It isn't easy at first. But we are all beginners when we initiate a journey. With each passing day, we build momentum, and it gets easier until it becomes second nature. The process itself becomes a healthy habit. I am not saying that I do not have bad days or feel negative emotions. Believe me, I do. The difference is, I recognize that I am having a moment and I let it happen.

I miss my mom so much that I can cry instantly sometimes when I think about her, which is every single day. But I have accepted her death because it's a part of life. I ride the waves of emotions, miss her ... feel gratitude for having had my mom for as long as I did, tell her I love her, and then I release their hold. Because it's another thing I have no control over, and choosing not to accept and move on is a form of suffering. Remember, suffering is a choice.

When I started my healing journey, I had no idea it was going to be this rewarding. I honestly thought I would heal my childhood trauma and move on. I didn't realize just how much healing I needed from my adulthood too. The amount of suffering I was putting myself through was killing my soul. I never realized how much release and happiness comes from forgiveness and acceptance. Forgiving myself had the biggest impact on my life. Forgiving my ex-husband was probably the most challenging, but I did it. No matter what I feel about any of the people from my past—good, bad, or ugly—I know I no longer have any anger toward them. I wish them all well.

As a life and health coach, I work with clients who need all sorts of things. I have specialized training in effective habit change so no matter what it is you want to change in your life, I can help. Simply changing your mindset to be more open-minded, positive, and less judgmental can change your life.

I have worked with individuals who were once just like I had been—unhappy, mentally and physically unhealthy, and at times, straight-up clueless. I work with individuals who make the hard choice to take control of their lives and stop playing victim to their circumstances. It's not for everyone. Unfortunately, there are more people in this world who choose to live in ignorance and choose to blame their problems on everyone BUT themselves. I help clients take control of their lives no matter what that means for them, though ultimately, it leads to greater happiness. Repeat clients are my favorites because they go deeper and really find themselves.

When I talk about myself, I often refer to "the old Jen and the new Jen." Old Jen was a people pleaser. She didn't have any personal boundaries. She allowed others to take advantage of her generosity and compassion, and she treated her mind, body, and spirit like shit. She was extremely unhappy, very uncomfortable in her own skin. She was highly insecure and sought out external validation. She settled. Settled for "just being a stay-at-home mom" and for a life of great unhappiness. And because of how low she felt about herself, she suffered through mistreatment from many individuals. She would allow others to manipulate her into feeling sorry for their "less-than" lives, and she would give expensive gifts and loan money to people who really deserved or needed something along the lines of a compliment or a listening ear. One of my coaches reminds me to remember "who deserves the car and who deserves the compliment."

Old Jen would go above and beyond to make others happy. She didn't realize she was subconsciously hiding behind helping others as a form of self-neglect. Don't misunderstand me when I say this because there are certain people in my life that deserved the gift or the financial help, while others were being greedy and taking advantage. And those people are no longer a part of my life. Those kinds of people have no place in my life.

New Jen is different. I treat my mind, body, and soul like the temple it is. I finally understand why we are instructed to put our oxygen masks on before helping anyone else. If we are not taking care of ourselves, we cannot really take care of anyone or anything else to our highest potential. I no longer seek external validation or pay any attention to the gossip and judgmental opinions of others. I have learned that people judge what they don't understand and what they fear. That most people are insecure and unhappy, and because of that, they cannot genuinely feel and show happiness for those around them. Even loved ones. As I said earlier, like attracts like. I express my boundaries and I enforce them in any way I need to. I no longer allow people to walk all over me.

I am learning that being overly generous to people with not only money but also time and energy is hurtful to me and, more often than not, backfires. I have learned that many people simply want the handout, and they do come back for more. New Jen doesn't put up with that. I no longer tolerate one-sided relationships and I no longer even associate with "energy vampires." I am learning the art of walking away from individuals, even ones that I love and share blood with, who are toxic and hurtful toward me.

My business name is **Jen's Life Coaching,** aka **JLC**. I know that isn't the most exciting name for a business because the name Jen is so common and basic to my generation. I went back and forth with creative names, and all of my coaches and even my branding expert explained to me that since I am selling myself and my coaching services, my name needs to be a part of it. When I realized that no other life coach named Jen took this simple and "boring" idea, I snatched up the domain name and created my brand.

I now refer to it as Jen's Coaching Empire because it branches off to 1:1 coaching, books, digital downloads, group coaching, and mastermind classes. I have a vision to help as many people to be intrinsically happy as I can. I love being happy and I love being around other happy people. We encourage and lift each other up while empowering each other to climb that next mountain.

We can't help everyone, but everyone can help someone.

Ronald Reagan

Nobody's Responsibility but Our Own

In nearly every culture, the dragonfly symbolizes change, metamorphosis, adaptability, and self-actualization. It is usually associated with developing a deeper and more authentic meaning of life. Dragonflies move with purpose, beauty, and grace.

I have loved dragonflies for as long as I can remember. I didn't even know much about them besides the symbolic meaning of transformation. I just liked their shape. Along with butterflies, I thought they were uniquely beautiful and different from other insects. Now I know why. It's no wonder I've adopted the dragonfly as part of my branding and logo design in my life coaching practice.

So what do I do exactly? To put it bluntly, I help women reclaim their independence and not take any crap from anyone, in an elegant and classy way. My clients' goals become my goals, whether I agree with them or not, because it is my goal to help them accomplish their goals.

Jen's Life Coaching helps people reclaim their independence. Financial independence and emotional independence. Freedom that comes from within ... intrinsically. *Not taking any crap* simply means knowing our boundaries and values, and holding true to them. We don't have to tolerate being mistreated, whether that means voicing our needs directly in a clear way or even, if necessary, cutting people out of our lives.

There is nothing wrong with eliminating unhealthy individuals from our lives. It doesn't mean we can't celebrate a special occasion with family, ex-relationships, or coworkers we no longer engage with on a regular basis. In fact, that action right there is the biggest accomplishment. Being able to attend my children's sporting events and celebrations AND sit next to their dad and his new wife with grace and class is such a gift to my children. And the best part is, I am not even faking it.

I don't know what their thoughts are, and that's not my business. We share children together, and our children deserve to have parents who are loving and supportive. I have said this to plenty of people who asked how my kids are doing after the divorce: they are happier than they have ever been.

This is where the resilience we talk about in previous chapters comes in. Children don't need their parents together to feel loved and supported. They need their parents to be happy. And if that means they are happier apart, then that is what is best for the kids, especially if the parents can get along. Divorce doesn't have to suck. It was one of the hardest things I have done in my life, and it was also one of my bravest. One of the best decisions I've made was leaving that entire dynamic. Doesn't mean either of us are bad people; it just means we aren't as compatible as we were when we got married. And that's okay.

Emotional freedom is letting go of anger and pain and the shit life throws at us with as much grace as we possibly can. Having freedom and independence over our past is another superpower, one we all have within us ... intrinsically. We don't have to be haunted constantly by our demons and horrible experiences we've gone through.

I am a perfect example of a person who has transformed her life from the inside out. My past *experiences* are, by far, not the worst that could've happened; so many others have gone through far worse. However, even though I have gone through nowhere near the level of trauma and fear that Anne Frank lived through while hiding from the Nazis in an attic, the kinds of feelings she described in her diary are the kinds of feelings I have had. The loneliness and constant state of fear, and even feeling ignored by a certain boy and highly disliking her mother. Or the feelings of disgust and shame that Jaycee Dugard felt before, during, and after being sexually violated for years in captivity. I never had a mother like Joan Crawford, but I can empathize with the anger and resentment one can feel toward a parent.

It's not a comparison about who had it worse. My point is, the *experience* itself is one aspect to consider, and while the experiences may differ vastly in terms of impact, the human feelings are the same.

And those feelings are what we need to heal, along with coming to terms with acceptance of what happened. So, while I was never as hurt and abused as many others on this planet, nonetheless, I was abused, repeatedly. It is comforting to know that I am not alone in my trauma-related emotions and subconscious defense mechanisms. None of us are alone.

Having made it to the other side of our traumatic experience(s) means we now have a choice. Our circumstances don't have to be a life sentence for misery. We can all get past these traumas and learn from them and live a happy life worth living that is in alignment with our passions, goals, and desires.

Happiness comes from within. Our happiness is nobody's responsibility but our own. And choosing happiness all starts with what we feed our minds, feed our bodies, and feed our soul.

So what do I do, exactly? To put it bluntly, I help women reclaim their independence and learn not to take any crap from anyone—in an elegant and classy way. My clients' goals become my goals, whether I agree with them or not, because it is my goal to help them accomplish their goals.

I owe the success I've achieved to myself, but I could never have done it without therapy and coaching.

I provide a range of life and health coaching services, including personalized life coaching based on your unique goals. If you are ready to do the work, I can help you unlock your transformation by providing guidance and keeping you on track in doing the things that will lead you to achieve your goals. Imagine waking up every day and being proud of yourself and loving the life you create. Having a life coach is a fantastic way to feel supported through your transformation.

If you would like to explore how I could be of help to you on your journey, please go to my website at www.jenslifecoaching.com.

About the Author

Jennifer is a certified health and life coach, and the author of her first book. Raised in Chicago, she now lives in sunny Florida with her three children. Jennifer is the founder and creator of Jen's Life Coaching, where she shares her passion for helping other moms live their best lives. She has a blog and a growing library of eBooks and eCourses on her website at jenslifecoaching.com, all designed to help moms achieve success—both professionally and personally. When she's not coaching or writing, you can find Jennifer spending time with her family, practicing yoga, or tinkering in her craft room, where she loves painting.

www.jenslifecoaching.com
www.jenniferwsterling.com

Bonus Chapter: Embracing Female Sexuality and Expression

ORIGINALLY PUBLISHED IN WOMANHOOD: IDENTITY TO INTIMACY AND EVERYTHING IN BETWEEN, EDITED BY KRYSTAL CASEY OF FLIGHT OF THE PHOENIX PUBLISHING.

This chapter originally appeared in the anthology *Womanhood: Identity to Intimacy and Everything in Between*. It's a deeply personal piece where I share my journey of overcoming sexual trauma and learning to embrace my sexuality and self-expression. Writing this was both healing and empowering for me, and I hope it inspires you to see your own power and potential for transformation. Special thanks to Krystal Casey and the amazing women who contributed to this anthology for creating such a powerful platform for these stories to be shared.

Are you ready to explore the forbidden?

I love sex. I am an unapologetic lover of all things sexual. I crave it, I embrace it, and I can indulge in it for hours with the right person. Gender doesn't matter to me; I've had sexual encounters with both men and women.

And the adventure continues! From total strangers to dear friends, and even those late-night connections, I've fearlessly delved into the depths of my desires. No shame, just pure exploration.

But I wasn't always like this. I used to feel ashamed of my sexuality and past traumas centered around it. I felt dirty, tainted, and broken. As much as I wanted sex and physical intimacy, part of me was repulsed by it. It felt more like a chore.

Today, I celebrate my inner vixen without shame or fear of judgment. I've embraced my sexuality, and it's empowered me to express myself fully and heal past sexual trauma in ways I never thought possible. It's where I find a deep connection with my femininity, a sense of freedom to be vulnerable and explore my desires without restraint.

In a world where taboos and stigma surrounding female sexuality persist, it is crucial for women to embrace their sexual authenticity. This chapter will examine the impact of societal taboos on female sexual expression, the benefits of healing sexual trauma, the profound connection between love and sex, and the importance of fostering trust and embracing unique expressions of love.

So, if you are ready to break free from the chains of society, unlock your true sexual self, and embark on a transformative journey of personal growth, read on to discover the key to embracing sexual authenticity.

Prepare yourself for an ultimate act of submission....to yourself.

Understanding the Impact of Societal Taboos & Stigmas

Sexuality: the enigmatic force that defines who we are. It's raw, primal, and yes, even a little wild. But here's the thing - it's perfectly natural. In fact, it's one of our fundamental needs as humans, and denying that is almost like denying ourselves air.

For centuries, women who were sexually active outside the confines of marriage were shamed and ostracized, often left to wear a metaphorical "Red Letter 'A'" to denote their supposed promiscuity. It's hard to forget Nathanial Hawthorne's controversial *The Scarlet Letter*, which portrayed an unmarried woman raising a child alone as sinful and morally corrupt for her sexual choices. She and her child were punished, shamed, judged, and isolated by her community for years.

A century later, the 1960s were a revolutionary time for women's sexual expression and empowerment. From the introduction of the birth control pill to an increase in women's participation in the workforce, women were no longer confined to strict gender roles. More importantly, women were able to express themselves without judgment or societal pressure. This era paved the way for future generations of women to continue to break down barriers and embrace their sexual empowerment.

Understanding the impact of societal taboos is essential when it comes to exploring female sexual expression and embarking on a journey of personal growth. These taboos have long held women back from fully embracing their sexuality and have created a barrier to healing from past traumas. By acknowledging and challenging these societal constraints, women can begin to regain their power and find the freedom to express love through sex in their own unique ways.

These stigmas surrounding female sexuality have also had a significant impact on the healing process for survivors of sexual trauma. In a society that often blames victims or shames them into silence, it can be incredibly challenging for survivors to find the support and understanding they need to heal. By breaking down societal taboos and creating a culture of empathy and acceptance, we can create a safe space for survivors to heal their wounds, so they can explore their sexuality and reclaim their bodies.

Slowly but surely, women are reclaiming their bodies and sexual experiences, and society has evolved enough to recognize and celebrate this. It's time to end the stigma of female sexuality and acknowledge the progress we have made. We still have a long way to go, but every step counts towards a world where women can be proud of and confident in their sexuality...trauma and all. It's empowering to see how far we've come and how much we still have the potential to grow. By embracing female sexuality and ending the stigmas that come with it, we're paving the way for a brighter, sex-positive future.

Sexual Trauma and the Effects on Intimacy

Sexual trauma is unfortunately all too common, with about 1 in 4 girls and 1 in 13 boys in the United States experiencing sexual abuse under the age of eighteen. According to Rainn.org, (Rape, Abuse & Incest National Network), America's largest anti-sexual violence organization, an American is sexually assaulted every 68 seconds.

Sexual trauma is a soul-shattering ordeal that scars us to the core. It leaves behind a deep-rooted mark on our sense of self and tampers with our ability to embrace our sexuality wholeheartedly. Tragically, countless survivors are imprisoned by shame and guilt, forced to endure their anguish in silence. The consequences? A cascade of darkness encompassing depression, anxiety, addiction, PTSD, migraines, obesity, and shattered relationships to name a few.

My Story

When I was between nine and fourteen years old, I was sexually abused by four men. The men would touch me inappropriately, and force me to perform sexual acts on them. The first one was a neighbor and husband of my mother's friend at the time. My mother was known for being too trusting, and her ability to judge character wasn't great.

The first time it happened, when he placed his hands between my legs to "warm them up," I instinctively knew something was wrong. I was petrified. We were in the car by ourselves, too terrified to tell him to stop. I moved to the passenger side and looked out the window at the sky, praying to get home quickly.

Instead, he took me to his parents' house, who were not home then. It was a few days from my ninth birthday, and he told me he needed to check my pants size to buy me some new clothes as a birthday present, and asked if he could unbutton them to look. I knew he was lying, but obliged to his request out of pure fear. I didn't want him to do this, yet I stayed silent. He pulled my pants down and quietly told me to lie on the bed. I laid down on my stomach, thinking that would protect my genitals from his advances. He didn't protest. He pinned me down, thrusting his rock-hard penis against my backside as he moaned with pleasure in my ear. I don't recall anything else after that moment, but it wasn't the last instance.

I finally found the courage to speak up and tell my mom. I vaguely remember that conversation. I don't think she believed me, because although he never touched me again, she didn't stop him from coming around me. Three other men hurt me after that. I never spoke up again, out of shame and fear, that I wouldn't be heard.

The impact of this trauma on my life has been truly overwhelming. It has left me battling anxiety, depression, weight gain, and post-traumatic stress disorder. And it has deeply affected my ability to connect intimately with others well into adulthood. It prohibited my sexual desires and created a barrier in sexual relationships.

The Journey Towards Sexual Healing

When we experience something traumatic, it can be tempting to try and push it deep down, hoping to forget and move on. However, repressing trauma is not a viable solution and can have long-lasting consequences.

The body and our subconscious are incredible organs that are hard at work even when we're asleep. They don't forget anything, no matter how much we try. Simply because we stop consciously thinking about it does not mean our bodies have moved on too. The unhealed trauma ultimately manifests in long-term side effects like headaches, anxiety, and depression. Therefore, it's essential to address our trauma head-on, no matter how challenging or painful it may be. We must allow ourselves to feel and confront our feelings to experience true healing.

The first step in embracing my sexuality was to let go of the shame and judgment that surrounded sex and my past. Society teaches us that women who enjoy sex are "sluts" and "whores," while men who do the same thing are praised as studs by all genders. It took a lot of self-reflection and unlearning these harmful beliefs, but once I did, I found that embracing my sexuality was incredibly liberating. I could experience pleasure on my terms and without fear of being judged.

Sexual trauma creates a wound that can linger long after the event has passed. It's like an uninvited guest that refuses to leave, taking up residence in our minds and hearts. But what if we could evict this guest through forgiveness? It may seem daunting and counterintuitive at first, but forgiveness has been shown to have a powerful healing effect on trauma survivors. By releasing our anger and resentment towards our perpetrators, we create space for healing and growth.

It doesn't mean we have to excuse their behavior or forget what happened, but it does mean we can move forward with greater peace and acceptance. Forgiveness can be a difficult process, but it is worthwhile and has the potential to transform our lives.

I endured the unbearable agony of forgiving the men who caused me harm. But the most heart-wrenching journey was forgiving my own mother who failed to shield me from such individuals due to her ignorance and neglect.

I empowered myself by embracing forgiveness. It allowed me to cultivate a sense of emotional and physical security with my partner and gave me the freedom to enjoy my sexual pleasure, both giving and receiving.

Education also plays a crucial role in healing sexual trauma. By educating ourselves and others about the nature of trauma and its effects on a person's sexuality, we can promote understanding and compassion. This includes learning about the various therapies and resources available to survivors, such as trauma-informed therapy or alternative healing practices like mindfulness and meditation. We can make a difference through advocacy, awareness, and actively confronting victim-blaming attitudes. Together, we can make real change and support those who have experienced trauma.

It can be difficult to navigate feelings of shame and guilt surrounding past experiences. If you've experienced trauma, it's important to remember that healing has no timeline. Taking things slow, seeking therapy, and open communication with your partner can all help create a safe and comfortable environment where you can explore your sexuality on your own terms and at your own pace.

Channeling Healing and Love Through Sexual Expression

Now let's talk about my favorite area of intimacy. The mind-blowing, and the most thrilling act of all. It lies in creating an electrifying, unbreakable connection with my partner. It is in this sacred realm where only we exist, a clandestine bubble where outsiders dare not enter. Our bond is forged through trust, love, patience, and the most intimate of connections. Here, we can express, explore, and indulge in pleasure. This is a place where our bodies and souls intertwine, where the healing of past and present takes place, fueled by its intoxicating power. Before healing my trauma, I could not experience this.

Sexual expression and intimacy can be powerful tools in healing past wounds and traumas when shared with a loving and understanding partner. As consenting adults, we have the right to decide what we do with our own bodies, and finding a partner who respects and supports that autonomy can be transformative. It's important to prioritize communication and understanding in any intimate relationship, and to approach sexual expression as a way to connect deeply with our partners and explore our own desires and healing journeys. By embracing intimacy in this way, we can cultivate a profound sense of healing, growth, and joy.

Non-conventional sexual practices such as BDSM, KINK, and sexual role-playing can also be beneficial in fostering intimacy and trust with our partners. These practices require a lot of communication, consent, and trust, which can deepen our connection and understanding of each other's needs. It's important to remember that these practices should never feel like an obligation, and should only be explored if both partners are fully comfortable and willing.

Furthermore, trust allows for the development of a shared language of consent and mutual understanding. Each partner's boundaries and comfort levels are respected, and consent becomes an ongoing and enthusiastic conversation. This creates a dynamic where consent is not just a one-time agreement, but a continuous process of checking in and ensuring both partners are fully engaged and comfortable. By fostering trust, couples can create a space to safely explore their sexual desires.

Embracing and honoring our sexuality can also help us build trust and intimacy with our partners. When we are open and honest about our needs and desires, we create a space for vulnerability and connection. Intimacy is not just physical; it's emotional, intellectual, and spiritual. Sex can allow us to connect more deeply and foster feelings of trust and security.

When it comes down to it, the most important thing to remember on your sexual journey is that your body belongs to you. It's important to embrace your sexuality in a way that feels true to yourself and your desires. Don't let anyone else's judgment or stigma hold you back from experiencing pleasure and forming meaningful connections with others.

In Closing

Sexual empowerment is an ongoing journey. While there is no one-size-fits-all approach to embracing womanhood and sexuality, it can be a necessary part of self-acceptance, trust, vulnerability, and connection. Sexuality is an integral part of who we are, and it's important to reclaim our story.

As women, we can counter the shame, judgment, and stigma put on female sexuality by embracing our desires and becoming agents of change in our own lives.

By learning to trust ourselves and communicate authentically and openly with others, we open up a world of possibilities for trusting relationships. It requires patience, open communication with our partners, self-reflection, and healing from past traumas. True sexual empowerment comes from within us and encourages feelings of freedom. By adopting a mindset of openness towards pleasure and exploration, plus letting go of judgment both towards ourselves and others, we can make great strides in this journey. Through self-acceptance and owning our power, we will find true sexual pleasure grounded in respect, consent, care, and love. Let's celebrate our freedom, honor each other's journeys, and create a culture of acceptance within ourselves and among others. Together, we can create a society where sexual liberation is the norm.

This chapter is part of the anthology *Womanhood: Identity to Intimacy and Everything in Between*, a collection of stories from 15 authors exploring themes of identity, intimacy, and healing. If you enjoyed this story, you can find more powerful narratives in the full anthology, available through Flight of the Phoenix Publishing or on Amazon.

Made in the USA
Columbia, SC
02 June 2025